WHEN
RELIGION
ISN'T
ENOUGH

WHEN RELIGION ISN'T ENOUGH

say Yes! to relationship

Mary Detweiler

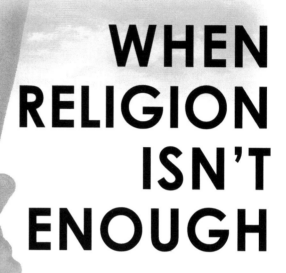

credo
house publishers

This book is dedicated to Jesus Christ,
who loves us so much he went to the cross for us.

Table of Contents

INTRODUCTION

I recently went to two funerals in two days. The first funeral was for a Christ follower who had accepted Jesus's invitation for a relationship. The second funeral was for a man who had been a lifelong Catholic. The contrast between the two funerals was, to me, a clear example of the difference between religion and relationship and led to my decision to write a second edition of this book. I wrote the first edition in 2012. That edition is now out of print.

The first funeral was a celebration and an expression of the man's relationship with Jesus. Though the family's loss and their consequent sadness was acknowledged with compassion, it was balanced with an abundance of joy. The joy was grounded in the knowledge that the man was with his Savior and that one day the family would be reunited in heaven, as all were followers of Christ. I walked out of that funeral as though walking on air with a heart full of hope and joy. It seemed clear to me that the pastor and family members who had planned that funeral had allowed themselves to be led by the Holy Spirit.

The second funeral was filled with the scripted liturgy of religion. I walked out of that funeral as though my ankles were being held down with weights and with a heart full of sadness. An image came to my mind of the Holy Spirit being strangled by the strict adherence to the liturgy. My sadness resulted primarily from two statements the priest made: (1) Everyone present could be assured that the man was in heaven because he had been baptized as an infant; and (2) Only those individuals who were Catholic were welcome to receive Holy Communion.

Those two statements of the priest distressed me because they directly contradict Scripture and because I know there are millions of people who believe these two statements.

Re: Baptism

Jesus preached that believing in him and trusting him is the only insurance one needs to spend eternity with God in heaven. "I tell you the truth, those who listen to my message and believe in God who sent me have eternal life. They will never be condemned for their sins, but they have already passed from death into life" (John 5:24). "Jesus told them, 'This is the only work God wants from you: Believe in the one he has sent'" (John 6:29). "Don't let your hearts be troubled. Trust in God, and trust also in me . . . I am the way, the truth, and the life. No one can come to the Father except through me" (John 14:1, 6).

Baptism is meant to be an outward sign of an inward commitment, a conscious decision to follow Jesus. It's the inward commitment, the decision, that ensures that one will spend eternity with God in heaven. Baptism does not ensure that.

"Then John [the Baptist] went from place to place on both sides of the Jordan River, preaching that people should be baptized to show that they had repented of their sins and turned to God to be forgiven" (Luke 3:3). The operative word here is *show*.

"Jesus came and told his disciples, 'I have been given all authority in heaven and on earth. Therefore, go and make disciples of all the nations, baptizing them in the name of the Father and the Son and the Holy Spirit'" (Matthew 28:18–19).

Important Point: Jesus's instruction to his disciples was to make disciples first. Baptizing them was to come second.

Re: Holy Communion

During his earthly ministry Jesus fed thousands of people on two separate occasions without asking them about their faith beliefs.

> Jesus saw the huge crowd as he stepped from the boat, and he had compassion on them because they were like sheep without a shepherd. So he began teaching them many things.
>
> Late in the afternoon his disciples came to him and said, "This is a remote place, and it's already getting late. Send the crowds away so they can go to the nearby farms and villages and buy something to eat."

But Jesus said, "You feed them."

"With what?" they asked. "We'd have to work for months to earn enough money to buy food for all these people!"

"How much bread do you have?" he asked. "Go and find out."

They came back and reported, "We have five loaves of bread and two fish."

Then Jesus told the disciples to have the people sit down in groups on the green grass. So they sat down in groups of fifty or a hundred.

Jesus took the five loaves and two fish, looked up toward heaven, and blessed them. Then, breaking the loaves into pieces, he kept giving the bread to the disciples so they could distribute it to the people. He also divided the fish for everyone to share. They all ate as much as they wanted, and afterward, the disciples picked up twelve baskets of leftover bread and fish.

A total of 5,000 men and their families were fed. Mark 6:34–44

About this time another large crowd had gathered, and the people ran out of food again. Jesus called his disciples and told them, "I feel sorry for these people. They have been here with me for three days, and they have nothing left to eat. If I send them home hungry, they will faint along the way. For some of them have come a long distance."

His disciples replied, "How are we supposed to find enough food to feed them out here in the wilderness?"

Jesus asked, "How much bread do you have?"

"Seven loaves," they replied.

So Jesus told all the people to sit down on the ground. Then he took the seven loaves, thanked God for them, and broke them into pieces. He gave them to his disciples, who distributed the bread to the crowd. A few small fish were found, too, so Jesus also blessed these and told the disciples to distribute them.

They ate as much as they wanted. Afterward, the disciples picked up seven large baskets of leftover food. There were about 4,000 men in the crowd that day, and Jesus sent them home after they had eaten. Mark 8:1–9

Also, at the last meal Jesus shared with his apostles he gave instructions to them as to how they were to remember him.

And he took bread, gave thanks and broke it, and gave it to them, saying, "This is my body given for you; do this in remembrance of me."

In the same way, after the supper he took the cup, saying, 'This cup is the new covenant in my blood, which is poured out for you.'" Luke 22:19–20 NIV

He did not instruct them to restrict anyone from participating in the Communion ritual.

I highly doubt he is pleased when clergy stop individuals from partaking of spiritual food. On the other hand, I believe he really likes a song by Sidewalk Prophets titled "Come to the Table." Lyrics:

We all start on the outside
The outside looking in
This is where grace begins
We were hungry we were thirsty
With nothing left to give
Oh the shape that we were in
Just when all hope seemed lost
Love opened the door for us
He said come to the table
Come join the sinners who have been redeemed
Take your place beside the Savior
Sit down and be set free
Come to the table
Come meet this mighty crew of misfits
These liars and these thieves
There's no one unwelcome here
That sin and shame that you brought with you
You can leave it at the door
And let mercy draw you near
So, come to the table

Come join the sinners who have been redeemed
Take your place beside the Savior
Sit down and be set free
Come to the table
To the thief and to the doubter
To the hero and the coward
To the prisoner and the soldier
To the young and to the older
All who hunger all who thirst
All the last and all the first
All the paupers and the princess
All who fail, you've been forgiven
All who dream and all who suffer
All who loved and lost another
All the chained and all the free
All who follow all who lead
Anyone who's been let down
All the lost you have been found
All who have been labeled right or wrong
To everyone who hears this song
Come to the table
Come join the sinners you have been redeemed
Take your place beside the Savior
Sit down and be set free
Come to the table

If any of this disturbs you or if you do not understand
the difference between religion and relationship, please
read on. I hope the difference, and the significance of the
difference, will become clear to you.

Important Note: When I speak of religion, I am not referring to any particular denomination or belief group. Throughout this book, whenever religion is mentioned, I am referring to "any system of rules, regulations, rituals, and routines that people use to achieve their spiritual end-goal."[1] Religion is about following rules. Relationship is about walking with God.

Chapter One

INVITATIONS AND PROMISES

"Are you tired? Worn out? Burned out on religion? Come to me. Get away with me and you'll recover your life. I'll show you how to take a real rest. Walk with me and work with me—watch how I do it. Learn the unforced rhythms of grace. I won't lay anything heavy or ill-fitting on you. Keep company with me and you'll learn to live freely and lightly." Matthew 11:28 MSG

From the beginning of time, God has invited the human beings he has created to be in relationship with him. His intention was never to give religion to the human race. His intention was to offer human beings a relationship with himself that was personal and intimate.

God's intention and desire for relationship seem fairly evident in his interactions with the first man and woman he created. "When the cool evening breezes were blowing, the man and his wife heard the LORD God walking about in the garden. So they hid from the LORD God among the trees. Then the LORD God called to the man, 'Where are you?'

(Genesis 3:8–9). Presumably, God wanted to walk with them in the garden. God changed his mind, however, when he discovered that the man and the woman had disobeyed him by eating the fruit of the one tree from which he had told them to eat no fruit. "So the Lord God banished them from the Garden of Eden, and he sent Adam out to cultivate the ground from which he had been made" (Genesis 3:23).

Though God deeply desires a personal and intimate relationship with each human being he creates, he does not force a relationship on anyone. He *invites* people to be in relationship with him, and he rejoices when one of his children responds to his invitation and enters into a relationship with him, becoming part of his family.

To listen to a wonderful song about how heaven rejoices when someone accepts God's invitation for relationship, go to http://www.youtube.com/watch?v=tSU q099PZhk, "Angels Are Dancing" by Sunday Shoes.

God's invitations

God's invitations are scattered throughout the Old and New Testaments.

In the Old Testament Solomon directs us to a relationship with God in the book of Proverbs.

> Trust in the Lord with all your heart;
>> do not depend on your own understanding.
> Seek his will in all you do,
>> and he will show you which path to take.

Don't be impressed with your own wisdom.
Instead, fear the LORD and turn away from evil.
Then you will have healing for your body
and strength for your bones.
Proverbs 3:5–8

Solomon was a man of great wisdom. He was King David's son and became king of Israel upon David's death. Fairly early in his reign as king "the LORD appeared to Solomon in a dream, and God said, 'What do you want? Ask, and I will give it to you!'" (1 Kings 3:5). Solomon's response was "Give me an understanding heart so that I can govern your people well and know the difference between right and wrong. For who by himself is able to govern this great people of yours?" (1 Kings 3:9). God was so delighted that Solomon had asked for wisdom instead of riches and fame that he gave him both what he had asked for (wisdom) and what he had not asked for (riches and fame). The book of Proverbs is a collection of Solomon's God-given wisdom.

The prophet Isaiah also points us toward a personal relationship with God. Isaiah is one of many prophets whose writings are contained in the Old Testament. Prophets were people chosen by God to be his mouthpiece on earth. God would give messages to the prophets, which the prophets in turn would deliver to the people of Israel. God spoke through Isaiah in the following verse, eloquently communicating his invitation for relationship: "So turn to me and be helped—saved!—everyone, whoever and wherever you are" (Isaiah 45:22 MSG).

Another of God's invitations is found in Psalm 146. The book of Psalms was Israel's prayer book and song book. Many, but not all, of the psalms were written by King David. The writer of this particular psalm beseeches us:

> Don't put your confidence in powerful people;
>> there is no help for you there.
> When they breathe their last, they return to the earth,
>> and all their plans die with them.
> But joyful are those who have the God of Israel
>> as their helper,
>> whose hope is in the LORD their God.
> Psalm 146:3–5

The clearest and most profound invitation, however, came when God sent his Son, Jesus, to earth. "For this is how God loved the world: He gave his one and only Son, so that everyone who believes in him will not perish but have eternal life" (John 3:16).

How to accept God's invitation

Accepting God's invitation for a relationship involves apologizing to God for behaviors and attitudes you engage in that are not in line with his values and then stopping those behaviors and attitudes and turning toward God— aka, repenting. Turning toward God means beginning to live your life his way, aligning your behaviors and attitudes with his values.

For many of us, this is a process. Though giving your life to God, entering into a relationship with him, accepting his free gift of forgiveness and salvation, deciding to live your life his way, and turning toward him is a once-in-a-lifetime decision, actually *living* your life his way is a lifelong process. Old habits die hard and usually don't give up without a fight. The more ingrained these attitudes and behaviors are, the longer it takes to change them and the more work and effort it will require. Once we are in relationship with God, however, the wonderful news is that we don't have to do it alone. He will be right there next to us, encouraging us, supporting us, and helping us.

John the Baptist told us how to accept God's invitation: "Repent of your sins and turn to God" (Matthew 3:2). When Jesus began his earthly ministry, he echoed John the Baptist's words, instructing us how to accept God's invitation: "From then on Jesus began to preach, 'Repent of your sins and turn to God, for the Kingdom of Heaven is near'" (Matthew 4:17).

If we accept God's invitation to enter into a relationship with him, he promises us the following:

God's promises

Moses communicated some of God's promises in Psalm 91:

> "If you'll hold on to me for dear life," says GOD,
>   "I'll get you out of any trouble.
> I'll give you the best of care
>   if you'll only get to know and trust me.
> Call me and I'll answer, be at your side in bad times;
>   I'll rescue you, then throw you a party.
> I'll give you a long life,
>   give you a long drink of salvation!"
> Psalm 91:14–16 MSG

God communicated many of his promises through Isaiah. Two of those promises are:

> I'll take the hand of those who don't know the way,
>   who can't see where they're going.
> I'll be a personal guide to them,
>   directing them through unknown country.
> I'll be right there to show them what roads to take,
>   make sure they don't fall into a ditch.
> These are the things I'll be doing for them—
>   sticking with them, not leaving them
>   for a minute.
> Isaiah 42:16 MSG

> When you're in over your head, I'll be there with you.
>   When you're in rough waters, you will not go down.
> When you're between a rock and a hard place,
>   it won't be a dead end—
> Because I am God, your personal God,
>   The Holy of Israel, your Savior.
> Isaiah 43:2–3 MSG

Jeremiah was another Old Testament prophet through whom God spoke on several occasions, communicating more of his promises. "If you look for me wholeheartedly, you will find me" (Jeremiah 29:13). "Call to me and I will answer you. I'll tell you marvelous and wondrous things that you could never figure out on your own" (Jeremiah 33:3 MSG).

When speaking to his disciples, Jesus summed up God's promises to take care of us. He said:

And don't be concerned about what to eat and what to drink. Don't worry about such things. These things dominate the thoughts of unbelievers all over the world, but your Father already knows your needs. Seek the Kingdom of God above all else, and he will give you everything you need. Luke 12:29–31

Chapter Two

GOD'S RELATIONSHIP WITH THE HUMAN RACE

The story of God's relationship with the human race is told in the Bible. "The story of the Bible is the story of God wanting us to come to him directly, offering us tools to help our relationship, and then watching broken-hearted as we fall in love with the tools, rather than God."[2]

After Adam and Eve left the garden, the human race grew and multiplied and became very evil.

> The LORD observed the extent of human wickedness on the earth, and he saw that everything they thought or imagined was consistently and totally evil. So the LORD was sorry he had ever made them and put them on the earth. It broke his heart. And the LORD said,

"I will wipe this human race I have created from the face of the earth. Yes, and I will destroy every living thing—all the people, the large animals, the small animals that scurry along the ground and even the birds of the sky. I am sorry I ever made them." But Noah found favor with the Lord. Genesis 6:5–8

God told Noah that he planned to destroy the evil human race with a great flood. God also told Noah that he intended to save Noah and his family from the flood. God then instructed Noah to build a boat, giving him the exact specifications, and Noah built the boat. God then told Noah to board the boat with his family and two of every species of bird, mammal, and reptile. "Noah did everything as the Lord commanded him" (Genesis 7:5). God then made it rain for forty days and forty nights. Floodwaters covered the earth, killing every living thing. God then brought wind, and the wind began to reverse the flood. When the flood waters receded, "Noah disembarked with his sons and wife and his sons' wives. Then all the animals, crawling creatures, birds—every creature on the face of the Earth—left the ship family by family" (Genesis 8:18–19 MSG).

The human race once again grew and multiplied. God then created a people who were set apart to belong to him, to be his family. God chose Abraham to be the father of his family. God promised Abraham that he would have many descendants and that these descendants would form many nations. Further, God promised Abraham that he would provide a home for his descendants. "This is the everlasting covenant: I will always be your God and the God of your descendants after you. And I will give the entire land of Canaan, where you now live as a foreigner, to you and your descendants. It will be their possession forever, and I will be their God" (Genesis 17:7–8).

God wants us to be as real with him as we are with our best friend. *Webster's Dictionary* defines friend as "a person on intimate and affectionate terms with another." That is the type of relationship God wants with each of us—an intimate, personal relationship.

Though God is our Friend, he is also our Father. In establishing and growing our relationship with God, we cannot overlook the parent-child aspect of the relationship. It is the core, indeed the very essence, of the relationship. "Now it came to pass, as He was praying in a certain place, when He ceased, that one of His disciples said to Him, 'Lord, teach us to pray, as John, also taught his disciples.' So He said to them, 'When you pray, say: Our Father . . .'" (Luke 11:1–2 NKJV).

One of the lenses through which one can read the Bible is the lens of God raising his children. God parents his children with love. Everything he does for us he does out of love.

God our Father

Those of us who are human parents know that there are many facets of parenting. We provide food, clothes, and shelter for our children. We also protect them from danger, teach them how to be a man/woman in the world, and discipline them when needed. It is no different with our heavenly parent. He provides for us, protects us, teaches us, and disciplines us when needed.

Important Note: Though God loves us with a perfect love, he does not always give us everything we want or let us get away with bad behavior. Like any good parent, he gives his children what they need, not what they want. Sometimes he says no to us, sometimes he lets us experience the consequences of our choices and actions, and sometimes he disciplines us. He doesn't discipline us because he's angry at us or disappointed in us. He disciplines us because he loves us.

Those of us who are human parents want many things for and from our children. One of the main things we want from our children is obedience, unquestioning obedience without discussion, negotiation, argument, and so forth. Is there a human parent alive who has not used the phrase "Because I said so!" when trying to get children to do something? I doubt it. If such a parent exists, I would like to meet him or her. The same holds true for God, our heavenly parent. He wants his children to obey him.

From the beginning of creation, God gave much to his children, and all he asked for in return was obedience. His children, right from the beginning, had a difficult time giving this to him. Think about it: God put Adam and Eve in the Garden of Paradise and told them they could have anything they wanted except for the fruit of one tree. So, what did they want? They wanted the fruit from that one tree. What did they do? They did what they wanted to do, not what they were told to do. Sound familiar? It certainly does to me.

Now think about this: when God told Noah to build a boat, Noah was in the middle of a desert! Can you imagine how ridiculous it must have seemed to the people around Noah that he was building a boat? Can you also imagine how much grief Noah and his family probably took because he was building a boat? Yet, Noah did not let anything deter him. He did what God told him to do because he loved God and trusted him. God wants this same kind of obedience from us. He wants us to obey him without question even when it seems to make no sense at all, *especially* when it makes no sense at all, and he doesn't take our disobedience lightly. Just as we human parents discipline our children when they disobey us, God disciplines his children when they disobey him. He disciplines, not punishes his children. To listen to a song by Colton Dixon about trust in God and obedience to God, visit https://www.youtube.com/watch?v=jjaKKAsQc34.

The word *discipline* comes from the same root as *disciple*, one who is taught. The goals of discipline are not justice, power, or revenge. True discipline has two purposes—education and behavior change. When we human parents discipline a child, we are attempting to teach that child self-control and respect for others and to replace negative behavior with positive behavior. The same holds true for our heavenly parent. When he disciplines us, he is attempting to teach us self-control and respect, and he is attempting to replace sinful behavior with godly behavior. This is addressed in the book of Hebrews in the New Testament.

And have you forgotten the encouraging words God spoke to you as his children? He said,

"My child, don't make light of the LORD's discipline,
and don't give up when he corrects you.
For the LORD disciplines those he loves,
and he punishes each one he accepts as his child."

As you endure this divine discipline, remember that God is treating you as his own children. Who ever heard of a child who is never disciplined by his father? . . . No discipline is enjoyable while it is happening—it's painful! But afterward there will be a peaceful harvest of right living for those who are trained in this way. Hebrews 12:5–7, 11

As previously stated, God chose Abraham to be the father of his family and promised Abraham that he would have many descendants and that he (God) would provide a home for these descendants. God also told Abraham, "You can be sure that your descendants will be strangers in a foreign land, where they will be oppressed as slaves for 400 years. But I will punish the nation that enslaves them, and in the end they will come away with great wealth'" (Genesis 15:13–14).

The foreign land Abraham's descendants would end up in was Egypt. When God was ready to bring his family, the Israelites, out of slavery in Egypt and back to Canaan, the land he had promised Abraham that he would give to his descendants, God chose Moses to lead them.

When the Israelites (about 600,000 men, plus all the women and children), left Egypt, "GOD kept watch all night, watching over the Israelites as he brought them out of Egypt" (Exodus 12:41 MSG). God never left them. He continued to keep watch over them and lead them on their journey. "God went ahead of them in a Pillar of Cloud during the day to guide them on the way, and at night in a Pillar of Fire to give them light; thus they could travel both day and night. The Pillar of Cloud by Day and the Pillar of Fire by night never left the people" (Exodus 13:21–22 MSG).

God protected his family

When word reached the king of Egypt that the Israelites had fled, Pharaoh and his officials changed their minds. "What have we done, letting all those Israelite slaves get away?" they asked. So Pharaoh harnessed his chariot and called up his troops. He took with him 600 of Egypt's best chariots, along with the rest of the chariots of Egypt, each with its commander. The LORD hardened the heart of Pharaoh, the king of Egypt, so he chased after the people of Israel, who had left with fists raised in defiance. The Egyptians chased after them with all the forces in Pharaoh's army—all his horses and chariots, his charioteers, and his troops. The Egyptians caught up with the people of Israel as they were camped beside the shore near Pi-hahiroth, across from Baal-zephon.

As Pharaoh approached, the people of Israel looked up and panicked when they saw the Egyptians overtaking them. They cried out to the Lord, and they said to Moses, "Why did you bring us out here to die in the wilderness? Weren't there enough graves for us in Egypt? What have you done to us? Why did you make us leave Egypt? Didn't we tell you this would happen while we were still in Egypt? We said, 'Leave us alone! Let us be slaves to the Egyptians. It's better to be a slave in Egypt than a corpse in the wilderness!'"

But Moses said to the people, "Don't be afraid. Just stand still and watch the Lord rescue you today. The Egyptians you see today will never be seen again. The Lord himself will fight for you. Just stay calm."

Then the Lord said to Moses, "Why are you crying out to me? Tell the people to get moving! Pick up your staff and raise your hand over the sea. Divide the water so the Israelites can walk through the middle of the sea on dry ground . . .

Then Moses raised his hand over the sea, and the Lord opened up a path through the water with a strong east wind. The wind blew all that night, turning the seabed into dry land. So the people of Israel walked through the middle of the sea on dry ground, with walls of water on each side!

Then the Egyptians—all of Pharaoh's horses, chariots, and charioteers—chased them into the middle of the sea. But just before dawn the Lord looked down on the Egyptian army from the pillar of fire and cloud, and he threw their forces into total confusion. He twisted their chariot wheels, making their chariots difficult to drive. "Let's get out of here—away from these Israelites!" the Egyptians shouted. "The Lord is fighting for them against Egypt!"

When all the Israelites had reached the other side, the Lord said to Moses, "Raise your hand over the sea again. Then the waters will rush back and cover the Egyptians and their chariots and charioteers." So as the sun began to rise, Moses raised his hand over the sea, and the water rushed back into its usual place. The Egyptians tried to escape, but the Lord swept them into the sea.

Then the waters returned and covered all the chariots and charioteers—the entire army of Pharaoh. Of all the Egyptians who had chased the Israelites into the sea, not a single one survived.

But the people of Israel had walked through the middle of the sea on dry ground, as the water stood up like a wall on both sides. That is how the Lord rescued Israel from the hand of the Egyptians that day. Exodus 14:5–16, 21–30

God provided for his family

Then the whole community of Israel set out from Elim and journeyed into the wilderness of Sin, between Elim and Mount Sinai. They arrived there on the fifteenth day of the second month, one month after leaving the land of Egypt. There, too, the whole community of Israel complained about Moses and Aaron.

"If only the Lord had killed us back in Egypt," they moaned. "There we sat around pots filled with meat and ate all the bread we wanted. But now you have brought us into this wilderness to starve us all to death."

Then the Lord said to Moses, "Look, I'm going to rain down food from heaven for you. Each day the people can go out and pick up as much food as they need for that day . . ."

That evening vast numbers of quail flew in and covered the camp. And the next morning the area around the camp was wet with dew. When the dew evaporated, a flaky substance as fine as frost blanketed the ground. The Israelites were puzzled when they saw it. "What is it?" they asked each other. They had no idea what it was.

And Moses told them, "It is the food the Lord has given you to eat. These are the Lord's instructions: Each household should gather as much as it needs. Pick up two quarts for each person in your tent."

So the people of Israel did as they were told. Some gathered a lot, some only a little. But when they measured it out, everyone had just enough. Those who gathered a lot had nothing left over, and those who gathered only a little had enough. Each family had just what it needed. Exodus 16:1–4,13–18

The end of the journey

When the Israelites arrived at the land of Canaan, Moses, per God's direction, sent a small group of men to scout out the land. After forty days they returned and gave the following report to Moses and all the Israelites:

"We went to the land to which you sent us and, oh! It *does* flow with milk and honey! Just look at this fruit! The only thing is that the people who live there are fierce, their cities are huge and well-fortified. Worse yet, we saw descendants of the giant Anak. Amalekites are spread out in the Negev; Hittites, Jebusites, and Amorites hold the hill country; and the Canaanites are established on the Mediterranean Sea and along the Jordan." Numbers 13:27–29 MSG

One of the members of the scouting party, Caleb, urged the Israelites to move forward and take the land. The others in the scouting party, however, discouraged this, saying, "It's a land that swallows people whole. Everybody we saw was huge . . . Alongside them we felt like grasshoppers. And they looked down on us as if we were grasshoppers" (Numbers 13:32–33 MSG). When the people of Israel heard this, the whole community erupted in weeping and wailing. They then rebelled against Moses and began planning to choose a new leader.

Caleb, along with Joshua, another member of the scouting party, stepped forward and addressed the entire community of Israel, saying:

> The land we walked through and scouted is a very good land—very good indeed. If GOD is pleased with us, he will lead us into that land, a land that flows, as they say, with milk and honey. And he'll give it to us. Just don't rebel against GOD! And don't be afraid of those people. Why, we'll have them for lunch! They have no protection and GOD is on our side. Don't be afraid of them! Numbers 14:7–9 MSG

The people reacted to Joshua's and Caleb's statements by threatening to stone them. God then appeared to Moses and asked, "How long will these people treat me like dirt? How long refuse to trust me? And with all these signs I've done among them!" (Numbers 14:11 MSG).

God disciplines his family

A fairly long dialogue then took place between God and Moses, in which Moses interceded for the people of Israel. God then instructed Moses to give the following message to the Israelites:

> "Your children, the very ones that you said would be taken for plunder, I'll bring in to enjoy the land you rejected while your corpses will be rotting in the wilderness. These children of yours will live as shepherds in the wilderness for forty years . . . You scouted out the land for forty days; your punishment will be a year for each day, a forty-year sentence to serve for your sins—a long schooling in my displeasure." Numbers 14:31–34 MSG

Throughout the forty long, difficult years in the wilderness, Moses trusted God, and God never abandoned him. God guided him and directed him as to what to do and when to do it. Each time the people complained and rebelled and disobeyed and God became angry with them, Moses intervened for the people, and God listened to him.

Chapter Three

THE BIRTH OF RELIGION

When the forty years came to an end, the people of Israel arrived, for the second time, at the land of Canaan, the home God had promised Abraham that he would provide for his descendants. When they arrived there, God told Moses he was about to die, and Moses, per God's instruction, commissioned Joshua to be his successor and lead the people of Israel into the promised land.

As they entered Canaan, the Israelites were faced with many walled cities full of enemies. Led by Joshua, they captured each of the cities one by one until they possessed the entire land, and they settled into their lives.

One would think that the Israelites, after all they had been through and all God had done for them, would have learned to trust God and obey him without question. Right? Wrong! They fell into a four-part cyclical pattern of (1) moving away from God and worshipping idols, (2) being conquered and enslaved by an enemy nation, (3) crying out to God for help and deliverance, and (4) God answering their call by sending a leader to bring them back to him. The people would then return to him for a while. This never lasted, though. They would eventually move away from him again, starting the cycle all over again. This cycle repeated itself over and over for many years.

God tried for a very long time to get his people back on track. He repeatedly sent leaders and prophets to help them and to warn them. Though the people responded to some of these godly leaders and returned to God, they never stayed there for very long. They continually drifted back into doing whatever they wanted, ignoring God's rules and expectations.

Note: In the original scrolls, these leaders and prophets are referred to as *shapat* (translation: judge). Shapat combines the ideas of "national leadership," "judicial decisions," and "political, military savior."[3]

Even King Solomon, who had been given great wisdom, drifted away from God late in his life and began to worship other gods. His disobedience did not happen overnight. It happened slowly and gradually. He began to drift away from God when he chose to love non-Hebrew women and marry them. When Solomon did this, he disobeyed one of God's commands: i.e., do not marry outside the faith. God issued this command due to the risk that foreign women would turn the hearts of the Israelites to other gods, and that's exactly what happened with Solomon. Like Adam and Eve, Solomon chose to do what he wanted rather than what God had told him to do.

As a result of Solomon's disobedience, God split the nation of Israel into two kingdoms when Solomon died. The northern kingdom was known as Israel, and the southern kingdom was Judah.

The residents of the northern kingdom continued to ignore God's commands and refused to live by his rules. God continued to try for a very long time to get them back on track. He continued sending judges to help them and to warn them. As before, some of these godly leaders were able to lead the Israelites back to God for a time; however, the people never stayed there. They continually drifted back into doing whatever they wanted, ignoring God's rules and expectations. God finally had enough and decided that the people of the northern kingdom, his children, needed serious discipline.

God disciplines his children again

To discipline them, God decided to exile his children in the northern kingdom to Assyria. This discipline was obviously very difficult and very painful, both for God and for the people. God expressed his pain through the prophet Hosea:

> "When Israel was a child, I loved him,
>   and I called my son out of Egypt.
> But the more I called to him,
>   the farther he moved from me,
> offering sacrifices to the images of Baal
>   and burning incense to idols.
> I myself taught Israel how to walk,
>   leading him along by the hand.

But he doesn't know or even care
    that it was I who took care of him.
I led Israel along
    with my ropes of kindness and love.
I lifted the yoke from his neck,
    and I myself stooped to feed him.

"But since my people refuse to return to me,
    they will return to Egypt
    and will be forced to serve Assyria.
War will swirl through their cities;
    their enemies will crash through their gates.
They will destroy them,
    trapping them in their own evil plans.
For my people are determined to desert me.
They call me the Most High,
    but they don't truly honor me.

"Oh, how can I give you up, Israel?
    How can I let you go?
How can I destroy you like Admah
    or demolish you like Zeboiim?
My heart is torn within me,
    and my compassion overflows.
No, I will not unleash my fierce anger.
    I will not completely destroy Israel,
for I am God and not a mere mortal.
    I am the Holy One living among you,
    and I will not come to destroy.
For someday the people will follow me.
    I, the LORD, will roar like a lion.

And when I roar,
    my people will return trembling from the west.
Like a flock of birds, they will come from Egypt.
    Trembling like doves, they will return from Assyria.
And I will bring them home again,"
    says the LORD.

Israel surrounds me with lies and deceit,
    but Judah still obeys God
    and is faithful to the Holy One."
Hosea 11:1–12

The people of Judah, however, didn't stay faithful to the Holy One for very long. They also fell into doing their own thing and ignoring God's commands. Approximately two hundred years after he had exiled the northern kingdom to Assyria, God exiled the southern kingdom (Judah) to Babylon.

This is what the LORD says:

"The people of Judah have sinned again and again,
    and I will not let them go unpunished!
They have rejected the instruction of the LORD,
    refusing to obey his decrees.
They have been led astray by the same lies
    that deceived their ancestors.
So I will send down fire on Judah,
    and all the fortresses of Jerusalem will be
    destroyed."
Amos 2:4–5

When God destroyed the fortresses of Jerusalem, the temple was also destroyed. The city lay in ruins.

Though God sent his people into exile, he did not abandon them. He continually sent messages of encouragement and hope to them, as well as promises of restoration, through the prophets Ezekiel, Isaiah, and Jeremiah. Some of these messages and promises are:

"Therefore, tell the exiles,
> 'This is what the Sovereign Lord says:
Although I have scattered you
> in the countries of the world,
I will be a sanctuary to you
> during your time of exile.'"
Ezekiel 11:16

"Do not be afraid, for I am with you.
> I will gather you and your children
> from east and west.
I will say to the north and south,
'Bring my sons and daughters back to Israel
from the distant corners of the earth.
Bring all who claim me as their God,
> for I have made them for my glory.
> It was I who created them.'"
Isaiah 43:5–7

"So do not be afraid, Jacob, my servant;
> do not be dismayed, Israel,"
> says the Lord.

"For I will bring you home again from distant lands,
> and your children will return from their exile.
Israel will return to a life of peace and quiet,
> and no one will terrorize them.
> For I am with you and will save you,"
> says the Lord.
"I will completely destroy the nations
> where I have scattered you,
> but I will not completely destroy you.
I will discipline you, but with justice;
> I cannot let you go unpunished."
Jeremiah 30:10–11

"Nevertheless, the time will come when I will heal Jerusalem's wounds and give it prosperity and true peace. I will restore the fortunes of Judah and Israel and rebuild their towns. I will cleanse them of their sins against me and forgive all their sins of rebellion. Then this city will bring me joy, glory, and honor before all the nations of the earth! The people of the world will see all the good I do for my people, and they will tremble with awe at the peace and prosperity I provide for them."
Jeremiah 33:6–9

"Give them this message from the Sovereign Lord: I will gather the people of Israel from among the nations. I will bring them home to their own land from the places where they have been scattered. I will unify them into one nation on the mountains of Israel. One king will rule them all; no longer will they be divided into two nations or into two kingdoms." Ezekiel 37:21–22

God eventually made good on his promises, as he always does, and brought an end to the disciplining process of the peoples of Israel and of Judah by providing a way for them to return to Canaan. Though he facilitated their return to their homeland, many Jews chose not to return. They remained scattered throughout the known world. The Jews who did return, particularly the leaders who returned, were determined to start over by not repeating the mistakes and sins of their past. The experience of having lived through war, destruction, captivity, and exile led many of them to embrace radical obedience as a major component of their faith. "The idea that right living would bring divine approval became an obsession among some religious people. . . . Their experience fortified their belief that the righteous will prosper but the wicked will perish."[4]

Could it be that this is where, when, and why relationship began to die and religion began to be born?

Good intentions

The people of Judah who returned to their homeland from exile had good intentions—they wanted to obey God. The mistake they made was that their desire to obey God was rooted in fear, not love.

Important Note: I realize that there are many verses in the Bible that tell us to fear the Lord, such as Proverbs 9:10: "Fear of the Lord is the foundation of wisdom." The fear that Solomon is referring to in the book of Proverbs, though, is not fear as in being afraid that we'll be hurt or being scared of a harsh punishment. It is more like awe or respect. God himself spoke of this kind of fear through the prophet Jeremiah: "Have you no respect for me? Why don't you tremble in my presence?" (Jeremiah 5:22). The writer of the book of Acts also spoke of this kind of fear when he said: "The story of what happened spread quickly all through Ephesus, to Jews and Greeks alike. A solemn fear descended on the city, and the name of the Lord Jesus was greatly honored" (Acts 19:17).

The fear that the people of Judah experienced when they returned to their homeland was not awe or respect, however; it was fear of a harsh punishment. They were afraid of what God would do to them if they didn't obey him. This is totally understandable in light of what they had been through—war, destruction, captivity, and exile. The problem with this, though, is that God wants us to obey him because we love him and trust him, not because we're afraid of him.

Reason for the rules

Those of us who are human parents give our children rules to live by because we love them. The rules provide needed boundaries, protecting and guiding them. In turn, we want our children to follow our rules because they love us and value the relationship they have with us, not because they are afraid of us. The same is true of our heavenly parent. When God gave the Israelites, his chosen people, his family, rules to live by, he was taking care of them, protecting them. He never meant for the rules to replace the relationship he had with them. He meant for the rules to *highlight* the relationship he had with them. He wanted the Israelites to be set apart from the nations surrounding them. He wanted them to live by a higher standard than their neighbors and to be identified to other nations as his people, his family. God did not want the Israelites to follow his rules so that they could *become* his children. They *already were* his children. God wanted them to follow his rules so that the world would *know* that they were his children.

Somewhere along the line the Israelites got the idea that they needed only to follow God's rules to be acceptable to him and to become part of his family. They forgot that, though he had sent them into exile, he had not ejected them from his family. He continued to be their Father. He was merely disciplining them for their misbehavior.

When the Israelites started misunderstanding the purpose of God's laws, and then started acting on the basis of that misunderstanding, religion was born. As a result of this misunderstanding, the Israelites shifted their focus from their relationship with God to the rules God had given them, putting their trust in the rules and in their own ability to follow them rather than putting their trust in God. Their view of God as a loving parent who would take care of them was replaced by a view of God as an angry parent who would punish them if they disobeyed him. Again, this is understandable in light of their experience of having been sent into exile. They moved from being dependent on God to being dependent on themselves. This is the very essence of religion.

Chapter Four

THE COVENANTS

A covenant is a "formal, solemn, and binding agreement." (Merriam-Webster Dictionary)

Throughout the history of his relationship with the human race, God entered into covenants with his people. When the flood was over, God promised Noah that he would never again send another like it and gave Noah a sign of his promise to keep that covenant.

> "I am confirming my covenant with you. Never again will floodwaters kill all living creatures; never again will a flood destroy the earth."

> Then God said, "I am giving you a sign of my covenant with you and with all living creatures, for all generations to come. I have placed my rainbow in the clouds. It is the sign of my covenant with you and with all the earth." Genesis 9:11–13

God's covenant with Abraham was discussed in chapter two. What was not discussed, however, was that God required a sign from the people to confirm their part of the covenant. "This is the covenant that you and your descendants must keep: Each male among you must be circumcised. You must cut off the flesh of your foreskin as a sign of the covenant between me and you" (Genesis 17:10–11).

God also entered into a covenant with Moses at Mount Sinai when he gave him the Ten Commandments (see Appendix One). It is this covenant God made with Moses that is commonly known as the Old Covenant.

Moses's explanation to the people of the blessings they would receive for obeying the commandments is found in the book of Deuteronomy, chapter 28. Also contained in that chapter is a listing of the consequences they would experience if they failed to keep the commandments.

Before he died, Joshua reminded them of all God had done for them. He spoke to them, giving them the following warning:

> So be very careful to love the LORD your God. But if you turn away from him and cling to the customs of the survivors of these nations remaining among you, and if you intermarry with them, then know for certain that the LORD your God will no longer drive them out of your land. Instead, they will be a snare and a trap to you, a whip for your backs and thorny brambles in your eyes, and you will vanish from this good land the LORD your God has given you. . . .

If you break the covenant of the LORD your
God by worshipping and serving other gods, his
anger will burn against you, and you will quickly
vanish from the good land he has given you.
Joshua 23:11–13,16

The Israelites made it abundantly clear that they
were unable to consistently live their lives in obedience to
God's commands, i.e., abide by their part of the covenant,
and God, as he always does, kept his promise and enforced
the consequences for their disobedience. He also began to
tell them, through the prophet Jeremiah, that he would be
replacing the old covenant with a new covenant he would
make with his people.

"The day is coming," says the LORD, "when I will
make a new covenant with the people of Israel
and Judah. This covenant will not be like the one
I made with their ancestors when I took them by
the hand and brought them out of the land of
Egypt. They broke that covenant, though I loved
them as a husband loves his wife," says the LORD.

"But this is the new covenant I will make with
the people of Israel after those days," says the
LORD. "I will put my instructions deep within
them, and I will write them on their hearts. I will
be their God, and they will be my people. And
they will not need to teach their neighbors, nor
will they need to teach their relatives, saying, 'You

should know the LORD.' For everyone, from the least to the greatest, will know me already," says the LORD. "And I will forgive their wickedness, and I will never again remember their sins." Jeremiah 31:31–34

The new covenant was established when Jesus died on the cross.

Why Jesus had to die on a cross

To understand why Jesus had to die on a cross, we need to go back to when the Israelites were set free from slavery in Egypt. One day as they were wandering in the wilderness, God said to Moses, "Have the people of Israel build me a holy sanctuary so I can live among them. You must build this Tabernacle and its furnishings exactly according to the pattern I will show you" (Exodus 25:8–9). God then proceeded to give Moses explicit directions down to the last detail as to how to build every inch of the tabernacle and every one of its furnishings and contents. He also gave Moses detailed instructions as to how the people were to worship him in the tabernacle.

One of the furnishings for the tabernacle was an altar upon which animals would be sacrificed as an offering to atone for sin. When the altar was finished, God told Moses, "Place the altar of burnt offering in front of the Tabernacle entrance" (Exodus 40:6).

God appointed Moses's brother Aaron and Aaron's sons to serve as his priests. God told Moses how and when to anoint and ordain Aaron and his sons, consecrating them to perform their priestly duties. One of these duties was the performance of the ritual in which animals were burned for the sin offering. Sin was considered to be "anything that violates one of the Lord's commands" (Leviticus 4:2). Once a person or persons sinned, the burnt offering was necessary in order to cleanse that person or persons of their sin and make them right with God.

The ritual of the burnt offering, as instructed by God to Moses, was as follows:

> "They must lay a hand on the head of the sin offering and slaughter it at the place where burnt offerings are slaughtered. Then the priest will dip his finger in the blood and put it on the horns of the altar for burnt offerings. He will pour out the rest of the blood at the base of the altar. Then he must remove all the goat's fat, just as he does with the fat of the peace offering. He will burn the fat on the altar, and it will be a pleasing aroma to the Lord. Through this process, the priest will purify the people, making them right with the Lord, and they will be forgiven." Leviticus 4:29–31

During one of the conversations between God and Moses, God explained to Moses why the killing of animals was necessary to atone for sin. He said: "For the life of the body is in its blood. I have given you the blood on the altar to purify you, making you right with the Lord. It is the blood, given in exchange for a life, that makes purification possible" (Leviticus 17:11).

47

The sacrificing of animals needed to be continually repeated because these blood sacrifices, or burnt offerings, atoned for sin partially and for a short time. When Christ shed his blood on the cross, however, it was a once-for-all-time sacrifice, making future sacrifices unnecessary. He was the Lamb of God, the perfect sacrifice God provided that would make all future sacrifices unnecessary. The blood of bulls and goats and lambs was no longer needed to cleanse people from their sin. Jesus's blood covers all who accept his free gift of salvation, forgiving all their sins—past, present and future—for all time.

The writer of the book of Hebrews in the New Testament stated, "If the first covenant had been faultless, there would have been no need for a second covenant to replace it" (Hebrews 8:7).

John Fischer, in his book *12 Steps for the Recovering Pharisee (Like Me)*, explains this quite clearly:

> The Old Covenant requires a standard of performance and a reason to be obedient to it. But the standard, in its truest form, is impossible to pull off consistently. It could be argued that this is the whole point of God's dealings with humanity through the covenants. The Old Covenant is there to break us, to show us that we cannot live according to its precepts—that sin and selfishness dwell in us to a significant degree so as to rule out the possibility of following even the clear call of Jesus to love God, self, and others. This inability to follow the standard, along with

its accompanying humility, qualifies us for a Savior—someone who will fulfill the law on our behalf and grant us righteousness as a free gift. This is God's grace as given to us in the New Covenant through the death and resurrection of our Lord and Savior Jesus Christ.[5]

Chapter Five

GOD SENT JESUS

God sent Jesus, his Son, to earth in a physical body to establish the new covenant and to restore what had been lost, a personal relationship between human beings and God.

As I imagine you know, God sent an angel, Gabriel, to visit Mary, a young woman in Nazareth who was betrothed to a man named Joseph. Gabriel told Mary, a virgin, that she was about to conceive a son by the Holy Spirit and that this child would be God's Son, the promised Messiah. When Joseph realized that Mary was pregnant, he resolved to end the relationship quietly.

> As he considered this, an angel of the Lord appeared to him in a dream. "Joseph, son of David," the angel said, "do not be afraid to take Mary as your wife. For the child within her was conceived by the Holy Spirit. And she will have a son, and you are to name him Jesus, for he will save his people from their sins." . . .

When Joseph woke up, he did as the angel of the Lord commanded and took Mary as his wife. Matthew 1:20–21, 24

Jesus was born in Bethlehem during the reign of King Herod. When Herod learned that a child had been born in Bethlehem who would be king of the Jews, he sent his soldiers to Bethlehem to kill every boy who was two years old or younger.

God protected his Son

An angel of the Lord appeared to Joseph in a dream. "Get up! Flee to Egypt with the child and his mother, the angel said. "Stay there until I tell you to return, because Herod is going to search for the child to kill him."

That night Joseph left for Egypt with the child and Mary, his mother, and they stayed there until Herod's death . . .

When Herod died, an angel of the Lord appeared in a dream to Joseph in Egypt. "Get up!" the angel said. "Take the child and his mother back to the land of Israel, because those who were trying to kill the child are dead."

So Joseph got up and returned to the land of Israel with Jesus and his mother. But when he learned that the new ruler of Judea was Herod's son Archelaus, he was afraid to go there. Then, after being warned in a dream, he left for the region of Galilee. So the family went and lived in a town called Nazareth. Matthew 2:13–14, 19–23

Jesus's earthly ministry

When Jesus began his earthly ministry, the first thing he did was choose companions who would be with him. These companions became his followers, or disciples. Out of these companions he chose twelve men who would be apostles. "One day soon afterward Jesus went up on a mountain to pray, and he prayed to God all night. At daybreak he called together all of his disciples and chose twelve of them to be apostles" (Luke 6:12–13).

Note: A disciple is one who follows, while an apostle is one who is sent.

Throughout the three years of his earthly ministry Jesus nurtured his relationship with the apostles. He taught them, encouraged them, and strengthened them so that they would be able to carry on his work after he was gone. He even continued to nurture and teach them after his death and resurrection.

The two primary aspects of Jesus's earthly ministry were healing and teaching. He healed the sick, the lame, the blind, the deaf, and those possessed by demons. At one point we are told that "as the sun went down that evening, people throughout the village brought sick family members to Jesus. No matter what their diseases were, the touch of his hand healed every one" (Luke 4:40).

He taught concepts that were new, different, and controversial. One of the most controversial concepts Jesus taught was that loving people is more important than obeying the law. The Jewish law at that time consisted of the Ten Commandments God had given Moses on Mount Sinai (see Appendix One) and more than two thousand laws Jewish religious leaders had developed to help people keep the Ten Commandments. One way Jesus modeled this teaching was by deliberately disobeying, and thereby challenging, their law that no work was to be done on the Sabbath.

> At about that time Jesus was walking through some grainfields on the Sabbath. His disciples were hungry, so they began breaking off some heads of grain and eating them. But some Pharisees saw them do it and protested, "Look, your disciples are breaking the law by harvesting grain on the Sabbath."

> Jesus said to them, . . . "You would not have condemned my innocent disciples if you knew the meaning of this Scripture: 'I want you to show mercy, not offer sacrifices.' For the Son of Man is Lord, even over the Sabbath!"
> Matthew 12:1–3, 7–8

The most important teaching

The most important and most controversial of his teachings was that following the rules will not get one to heaven. After all, this was central to his whole purpose for coming to earth in human form. He continually told people that the way to God and to eternal life is not religion (i.e., obeying the law); it is relationship (believing that he was who he said he was, the Son of God, and following him). He continually pointed to himself as the way to heaven. When speaking with his disciple Nathanael, "he said, 'I tell you the truth, you will all see heaven open and the angels of God going up and down on the Son of Man, the one who is the stairway between heaven and earth'" (John 1:51). When talking to Martha, Lazarus's sister, Jesus said: "'I am the resurrection and the life. Anyone who believes in me will live, even after dying. Everyone who lives in me and believes in me will never ever die'" (John 11:25–26). When speaking to the religious leaders, Jesus said: "'You search the Scriptures because you think they give you eternal life. But the Scriptures point to me! Yet you refuse to come to me to receive this life'" (John 5:39–40). Five days before his death Jesus said the following words to a crowd in Jerusalem: "'If you trust me, you are trusting not only me, but also God who sent me. For when you see me, you are seeing the one who sent me. I have come as a light to shine in this dark world, so that all who put their trust in me will no longer remain in the dark'" (John 12:44–46). At the last meal Jesus shared with the apostles before his death, he again made the point that trusting in him, not in a set of rules or laws, is the way to God. He said:

"'Don't let your hearts be troubled. Trust in God, and trust also in me . . . . I am the way, the truth, and the life. No one can come to the Father except through me.'" John 14:1, 6

All about love

Jesus's entire earthly ministry was characterized by love. He preached it and lived it. His final act of love for humanity, while he was still in his earthly body, was allowing himself to be crucified. He understood that the ultimate purpose for which he had come to earth was to offer himself as a sacrifice for all the sins and wrongdoings of all humankind, thus giving the children of God the opportunity to transition from religion (the old covenant) to relationship (the new covenant). Throughout the three years of his earthly ministry, he never lost sight of that purpose. As he went about ministering to people by teaching them and healing them, he was always moving toward the fulfillment of his ultimate purpose. "Jesus went through the towns and villages, teaching as he went, always pressing on toward Jerusalem" (Luke 13:22).

If you want a picture of pure, perfect love, picture Jesus, bloody and beaten beyond recognition and hanging on a wooden cross. He did not have to stay hanging there. He *chose* to stay hanging there. It was not nails that held him to that cross. It was love, love for each and every one of us, past, present and future, including the people who had crucified him and those who mocked and abused him as he hung on the cross.

The people passing by shouted abuse, shaking their heads in mockery. "Look at you now!" they yelled at him. "You said you were going to destroy the Temple and rebuild it in three days. Well then, if you are the Son of God, save yourself and come down from that cross!"

The leading priests, the teachers of religious law, and the elders also mocked Jesus. "He saved others," they scoffed, "but he can't save himself! So he is the King of Israel, is he? Let him come down from that cross right now, and we will believe in him! He trusted God, so let God rescue him now if he wants him! For he said, 'I am the Son of God.'" Matthew 27:39–43

What the priests, teachers of religious law, and elders didn't understand was that Jesus stayed on that cross because he loved them. If Jesus had come down from that cross, which he was more than capable of doing, he would not have given them and us the opportunity to transition from religion (the old covenant) to relationship (the new covenant). He would not have become the stairway between heaven and earth.

The veil

The definitive sign that Jesus had completed the work he had come to earth to do, i.e., restore the relationship that had been lost between God and humanity, was that at the moment of his death the veil in the temple in Jerusalem ripped in half. "And Jesus cried out with a loud voice, and breathed His last. Then the veil of the temple was torn in two, from top to bottom" (Mark 15:37–38 NKJV).

The significance of the veil in the temple tearing at the moment of Jesus's death is lost on many twenty-first-century churchgoers. To first-century Jews who believed that Jesus was the Messiah, however, the significance was enormous. The tearing of the veil meant that individuals now had direct access to God. They no longer needed a priest to act as an intermediary.

To understand the significance to first-century Jews, we need to go back to when God gave Moses the directions for the tabernacle and its contents. When God began to instruct Moses how to build the temple's furnishings and contents, the first set of plans he gave Moses were for an ark. "Have the people make an Ark of acacia wood—a sacred chest 45 inches long, 27 inches wide, and 27 inches high . . . When the Ark is finished, place inside it the stone tablets inscribed with the terms of the covenant, which I will give you" (Exodus 25:10, 16).

God then told Moses,

"You shall make a veil woven of blue, purple, and scarlet thread, and fine woven linen. It shall be woven with an artistic design of cherubim. You shall hang it upon the four pillars of acacia wood overlaid with gold. Their hooks shall be gold, upon four sockets of silver. And you shall hang the veil from the clasps. Then you

shall bring the ark of the Testimony in there, behind the veil. The veil shall be a divider for you between the holy place and the Most Holy."
Exodus 26:31–33 NKJV

When the tabernacle and all its contents were completed, Moses set up the tabernacle according to God's instructions. He hung the veil between the Holy Place and the Most Holy Place, and he put the two stone tablets on which were inscribed the commandments God had given Moses on Mount Sinai inside the Ark of the Covenant. He then placed the ark in the Most Holy Place.

God made it clear to Moses that Aaron and his sons, as the priests, would be the only ones who were to enter the Holy Place. Further, Aaron, as the high priest, would be the only one allowed to enter the Most Holy Place, and he could enter it only once a year on the Day of Atonement. The people could draw only so close to God. The priests would then cover the distance between the people and God, acting as the intermediary representing the people before God.

Since the Israelites were on a journey, the tabernacle needed to be able to move with them. Therefore, God gave Moses explicit instructions as to how to break down the tabernacle, pack all its contents, and move it. The tabernacle traveled with the Israelites throughout all the years they wandered in the wilderness. When the Israelites crossed the Jordan River into the promised land, they took the tabernacle with them. While the Israelite army was taking possession of each of the enemy cities, their main camp was at Gilgal. The tabernacle most likely remained at

Gilgal until all the cities were conquered. It was then moved to Shiloh, where it remained throughout the three hundred or so years the Israelites went through their cyclical pattern of moving away from and returning to God. When David became king, he retrieved the Ark of the Covenant and brought it to Jerusalem.

When King Solomon built the permanent tabernacle (the temple) in Jerusalem, the Ark of the Covenant was placed in the inner sanctuary of the temple, the Most Holy Place. As previously stated, the temple was destroyed when God exiled the southern kingdom (Judah) to Babylon. When King Cyrus of Persia conquered the Babylonian empire, he permitted the people of Judah to return to Jerusalem and rebuild the temple. King Cyrus was succeeded by King Darius, who supported the rebuilding of the temple. It was completed during the sixth year of his reign.

This is the temple that was standing in Jerusalem at the time of Jesus's death. When God tore the veil in the temple, he was, in essence, inviting people to come to him directly and enter into relationship with him. They no longer needed priests to act as intermediaries. Each individual now had direct access to God, if he or she wanted it.

The invitation still stands

God's invitation to enter into relationship with him still stands. Though God deeply desires a relationship with every human being he creates, he is respectful. He does not force himself on us. He doesn't demand or coerce. He invites.

It is important to remember that every one of us needs to make a decision whether to accept or reject God's invitation. It is also important to remember that not making a decision is, in essence, rejecting God's invitation for a relationship.

In his letter to the church in Rome, the apostle Paul urged the people of that church to accept God's invitation by committing their lives to Christ: "And so, dear brothers, I plead with you to give your bodies to God. Let them be a living sacrifice, holy—the kind he can accept. When you think of what he has done for you, is this too much to ask?" (Romans 12:1 TLB).

Paul is telling them, and us, what it means to commit our lives to Christ and how to do this. When he says "give your bodies to God," he is saying that God wants all of each one of us. Paul was telling them, and is telling us, that God doesn't want only what we choose to give him; he wants his creation back in its entirety. God created each one of us for a specific purpose, and he equipped us to fulfill that purpose. What he wants in return is for each of us to surrender ourselves to him and allow him to use us as he chooses.

When Paul said, "Let them be a living [and holy] sacrifice," he was explaining to the Christians in Rome that what is required under the new covenant is markedly different from what had been required under the old covenant. Paul was telling them that God no longer wants a dead sacrifice—i.e., animals burned on the altar of the tabernacle. God now wants a living sacrifice. He wants us to give him *our selves* so he can use us to further his work in the world.

Paul reminds us of the sacrifice God made for all of us (Christ's death on the cross) when he says, "When you think of what he has done for you, . . ." Paul was reminding his audience that God gave his only Son to experience a death marked by a degree of agony that few, if any, of us could even come close to imagining. Paul goes on to challenge both them and us with "Is this too much to ask?"

Editorial Comment: When you really think about the sacrifice Jesus made for us (he left the glory of heaven to enter the world in a human body and then allowed himself to be beaten beyond recognition, mocked, abused, and left to die a slow, tortuous death on a wooden cross), is our full surrender indeed too much to ask?

Chapter Six

NURTURING THE RELATIONSHIP

If one chooses to accept God's invitation for relationship, he or she must nurture that relationship if it is to be healthy and vibrant. Just as plants need to be nurtured with sun and water to stay alive and to grow, our relationship with God needs to be nurtured to stay alive and to grow. The sun and water of our relationship with God are prayer and worship.

Prayer is the sun

Jesus is our primary model for developing and maintaining a healthy prayer life. Throughout his earthly ministry Jesus frequently spent time with his Father in prayer. This was what kept him going. It gave him the fuel he needed to carry out his mission on earth. "As often as possible Jesus withdrew to out-of-the-way places for prayer" (Luke 5:16 MSG).

When Jesus prayed, he talked to his Father the way any one of us would talk to someone we trusted, respected, and cared deeply about. He did not recite memorized words and phrases. He told his Father how he felt and what he needed. For example, when Jesus arrived at the tomb of his friend Lazarus, he told those who were present to roll the stone aside from the entrance to the tomb.

So they rolled the stone aside. Then Jesus looked up to heaven and said, "Father, thank you for hearing me. You always hear me, but I said it out loud for the sake of all these people standing here, so that they will believe you sent me." Then Jesus shouted, "Lazarus, come out!" And the dead man came out, his hands and feet bound in graveclothes, his face wrapped in a headcloth. Jesus told them, "Unwrap him and let him go!" John 11:41–44

Another example of Jesus engaging in authentic dialogue with his Father was when he prayed in the Garden of Gethsemane immediately prior to his arrest:

"Father, if you are willing, please take this cup of suffering away from me. Yet I want your will to be done, not mine." Then an angel from heaven appeared and strengthened him. He prayed more fervently, and he was in such agony of spirit that his sweat fell to the ground like great drops of blood. Luke 22:42–44

Jesus was real with his Father. He did not pretend to feel something he did not feel, nor did he minimize how he was feeling. This is an example to us. God wants us to be as real with him as Jesus was.

A different experience

Growing up, my experience of prayer was very different from what Jesus modeled. I was taught to memorize prayers someone else had written and then to recite those prayers at specified times during liturgies. As these prayers were never explained to me, I had no understanding of what the words and phrases I was reciting meant. I was not connected to these prayers in any way. The entire experience of praying was empty and meaningless to me.

As my personal relationship with God grew and developed, I began to see prayer in a new and very different light. I began to experience prayer as a relational dialogue. I could talk to the God of the universe, and he talked to me! What an awesome privilege! He actually cared enough about me and my life to listen and respond.

Note: God's communications to me did not come in the form of audible words. They came in a multitude of other forms. Sometimes they would come as internal promptings and feelings. Other times they would come in the form of words practically jumping off a page at me as I read the Bible, or words of a worship song I was listening to touching me in a deep and powerful way. At still other times God chose to speak to me through people. Regardless of the form God's communications came in, each one was accompanied by a sensing or a knowing in the very fiber of my being that God was telling me something.

Learning to pray

As I worked at developing my prayer life, I encountered several difficulties and obstacles. First of all, due to my childhood experience of prayer I was resistant to formulas for prayer. I was afraid that I would be put into a religious straitjacket. I did not want my prayer life to be another empty exercise. I wanted it to be real and vibrant. Though I wanted this and indeed yearned for it, I was also afraid of it. I had not experienced this kind of authentic dialogue growing up in my family and, therefore, as I moved into adulthood engaging in a dialogue in which I could be totally honest and vulnerable was not familiar to me or comfortable for me. I struggled with this in both my human relationships and in my relationship with God.

As I got to know God and understand his character, though, I was able to see the differences between my heavenly parent and my earthly parents. I came to realize and believe that though my earthly parents had not engaged in this kind of authentic dialogue with me, my heavenly parent was different. He wanted authentic dialogue, not superficial chatter.

Another obstacle I encountered as I was learning to pray was truly believing that prayer moves the hand of God. Though I wanted to believe this, down deep inside me I really did not believe that my prayers made a difference to God at all, that they would have any impact on what he chose to do or not do. Not only did I have difficulty believing that my prayers could move the hand of God, I felt guilty for having difficulty believing this. My guilt decreased somewhat when I read the following Scripture passage from the book of Acts:

> Herod . . . arrested Peter . . . Then he imprisoned him, placing him under the guard of four squads of four soldiers each. Herod intended to bring Peter out for public trial after the Passover. But while Peter was in prison, the church prayed very earnestly for him.
>
> The night before Peter was to be placed on trial, he was asleep, fastened with two chains between two soldiers. Others stood guard at the prison gate. Suddenly, there was a bright light in the cell, and an angel of the Lord stood before Peter. The angel struck him on the side to awaken him and said, "Quick! Get up!" And the chains fell off his wrists. Then the angel told him, "Get dressed and put on your sandals." And he did. "Now put on your coat and follow me," the angel ordered.
>
> So Peter left the cell, following the angel. But all the time he thought it was a vision. He didn't realize it was actually happening. They passed the first and second guard posts and came to the iron gate leading to the city, and this opened for them all by itself. So they passed through and started walking down the street, and then the angel suddenly left him.

Peter finally came to his senses. "It's really true!" he said. "The Lord has sent his angel and saved me from Herod and from what the Jewish leaders had planned to do to me!"

When he realized this, he went to the home of Mary, the mother of John Mark, where many were gathered for prayer. He knocked at the door in the gate, and a servant girl named Rhoda came to open it. When she recognized Peter's voice, she was so overjoyed that, instead of opening the door she ran back inside and told everyone, "Peter is standing at the door!"

"You're out of your mind!" they said. When she insisted, they decided, "It must be his angel."

Meanwhile, Peter continued knocking. When they finally opened the door and saw him, they were amazed. Acts 12:3–16

Question: Why didn't those in the house praying believe Rhoda? Why were they amazed when they saw Peter standing at the door? Scripture tells us that they had been praying for him. I imagine that many, if not all, of the prayers were for his release. When Rhoda told them that Peter was standing at the door, why didn't they reply "Of course he is. We've been praying for this"? Could it be that they also did not fully believe in the power of prayer?

I don't know who all was gathered at the home of Mary, the mother of John Mark; however, I have to believe that at least some of those who were gathered there had known Jesus in the flesh. Some may very well have even traveled with him. So, when I think of my difficulty believing in the power of prayer, I am comforted by the knowledge that even people who knew Jesus in the flesh and probably watched him praying and probably listened to his teachings on prayer also had trouble believing in the power of prayer.

Any of you reading this who have had or are still having difficulty believing that prayer moves the hand of God, I hope that you can take some comfort in knowing that you are in good company.

More encouragement

I was further encouraged and emboldened when I read the following words of Jesus to his disciples as he was teaching them about prayer:

"And so I tell you, keep on asking, and you will receive what you ask for. Keep on seeking, and you will find. Keep on knocking, and the door will be opened to you. For everyone who asks, receives. Everyone who seeks, finds. And to everyone who knocks, the door will be opened.

"You fathers—if your children ask for a fish, do you give them a snake instead? Or if they ask for an egg, do you give them a scorpion? Of course not! So if you sinful people know how to give good gifts to your children, how much more will your heavenly Father give the Holy Spirit to those who ask him." Luke 11:9–13

I decided to take Jesus at his word and do what he was telling us to do. I began to ask God for the desires of my heart and tell him anything and everything that was on my mind. Though I have not received everything I have asked for, I trust that God hears me and, as a good parent, considers everything that I ask for and answers my prayers in the way that he deems best for me.

Bill Hybels's words in *Too Busy Not to Pray* further bolstered my efforts to learn to pray. He said: "The important thing is not to follow a particular method but to find a way that works for you. Custom-design an approach that will still your racing mind and body, soften your heart and enable you to hear God's still, small voice. Then, when you are centered and focused on God, invite him to speak to you."[6]

I decided to heed Bill Hybels's advice and began to experiment with various ways to pray. I let go of my belief that there is a "right" way to pray—i.e., a "right" posture (kneeling), "right" words (a pre-written prayer), a "right" time" (first thing in the morning), and so forth. I embraced the belief that God doesn't care how I talk to him or when I talk to him. What he cares about is *that* I talk to him. I tried praying at different times during the day and in different places. I eventually found that, though I had times with God when I would sit quietly in his presence, what worked the best for me was to have an ongoing dialogue with him throughout each day as I lived my life. I began to talk to God while I was driving, walking, working, doing chores around the house, sitting on a bench in the mall waiting for one of my children, and so forth. The possibilities were endless. I was reminded of Paul's words to the church in Thessalonica: "Pray without ceasing" (1 Thessalonians 5:17 NKJV).

I also found an additional role model for prayer. I began to look to Hannah in the Old Testament as another model for how to pray.

> Once after a sacrificial meal at Shiloh, Hannah got up and went to pray. Eli the priest was sitting at his customary place beside the entrance of the Tabernacle. . . .
>
> As she was praying to the LORD, Eli watched her. Seeing her lips moving but hearing no sound, he thought she had been drinking. "Must you come here drunk?" he demanded. "Throw away your wine!"
>
> "Oh no, sir!" she replied. "I haven't been drinking wine or anything stronger. But I am very discouraged, and I was pouring out my heart to the LORD." 1 Samuel 1:9, 12–15

The more I poured out my heart to God as Hannah did, the more he responded to me. As this exchange repeated itself over and over again, my relationship with God became more vibrant, firmly rooting itself in the center of my life. I began to see prayer not as an activity but rather as a lifestyle. An ongoing dialogue with God wove itself into the very fabric of my daily life and became as automatic to me as breathing. My need to stay connected to God became as much a basic need as eating, sleeping, and breathing. Over the years I have come to depend on him to keep me going as much as I depend on air and water to keep me living. It is the time I spend with God in prayer that breathes life into my relationship with him, and because he has consistently sustained me and provided for me, I can't help but worship him.

Bill Hybels puts it this way: "Prayer is the way to turn dry, theological descriptions into warm, living, personal realities. When we live in constant communion with God, our needs are met, our faith increases, our love expands. We begin to feel God's peace in our hearts, and we spontaneously worship him."[7]

Worship is the water

As previously stated, King David retrieved the Ark of the Covenant and brought it to Jerusalem. When the ark entered the city of Jerusalem, "David danced before the LORD with all his might, wearing a priestly garment" (2 Samuel 6:14).

Though David was far from perfect, he loved God with all his heart, and that love spilled out when the ark entered Jerusalem. He was so full of joy to see the ark entering the Israelite capital city that his joy could not be contained, and he danced (i.e., worshipped) "with all his might."

King David's worship was exuberant. It was fueled by his relationship with God and was a reflection of that relationship. It was also fueled by his understanding of the significance of the ark and his gratitude for what God had done for his people, the Israelites, through the ark.

Role of the ark

When the Israelites' time of wandering in the wilderness came to an end and they arrived at Canaan for the second time, the ark played a significant role in the peoples' crossing of the Jordan River into the promised land.

"In the morning Joshua said to the priests, 'Lift up the Ark of the Covenant and lead the people across the river.' And so they started out and went ahead of the people" (Joshua 3:6). Joshua then said to the people:

> "Look, the Ark of the Covenant, which belongs to the Lord of the whole earth, will lead you across the Jordan River! . . . The priests will carry the Ark of the LORD, the Lord of all the earth. As soon as their feet touch the water, the flow of the water will be cut off upstream, and the river will stand up like a wall."

> So the people left their camp to cross the Jordan, and the priests who were carrying the Ark of the Covenant went ahead of them. It was the harvest season, and the Jordan was overflowing its banks. But as soon as the feet of the priests who were carrying the Ark touched the water at the river's edge, the water above that point began backing up a great distance away at a town called Adam, which is near Zarethan. And the water below

that point flowed on to the Dead Sea until the riverbed was dry. Then all the people crossed over near the town of Jericho.

Meanwhile, the priests who were carrying the Ark of the LORD's Covenant stood on dry ground in the middle of the riverbed as the people passed by. They waited there until the whole nation of Israel had crossed the Jordan on dry ground. Joshua 3:11, 13–17

And when everyone was safely on the other side, the priests crossed over with the Ark of the LORD as the people watched . . .

As soon as the priests carrying the Ark of the Lord's Covenant came up out of the riverbed and their feet were on high ground, the water of the Jordan returned and overflowed its banks as before. Joshua 4:11, 18

The ark also played a significant role in the conquering of each of the walled cities. While the tabernacle most likely remained at Gilgal during this process, the ark traveled with the Israelites.

Other reactions

Not everyone worshipped and rejoiced as David did when the ark entered Jerusalem. David's wife, Michal, did not share in his joy. Rather than participating in the joyous worship, Michal judged David's behavior and reacted with loathing. "But as the Ark of the LORD entered the City of David, Michal, the daughter of Saul, looked down from her window. When she saw King David leaping and dancing before the LORD, she was filled with contempt for him" (2 Samuel 6:16).

What fueled Michal's reaction is a matter of speculation and is beyond the scope of this book. What is within the bounds of this book, however, is the reality that, though this scenario occurred many centuries ago, I have seen the same dynamic at play in churches and at worship services today. I have watched as some people worshipped God with joy and abandon, while others looked at them with discomfort and/or disdain.

For a long time I allowed these looks of discomfort and disdain to stop me from freely worshipping God during a worship service. In order to get past this and become free to worship during a church service, I had to come face-to-face with my codependent characteristic of caring about what people think of me and basing my opinion of myself on my perception of others' opinions about me. I not only had to come face-to-face with this character trait, I had to overcome it and not let it rule me. I overcame it by continually reminding myself that I am living my life for an audience of One and that his opinion of me is the only opinion that matters.

It is the time I spend worshipping God as the Spirit moves me that pumps blood into my relationship with him. I believe that God smiles when we allow ourselves to be who he created us to be. So, when I worship him freely in a worship service, whether that be standing or sitting or with hands raised or in my lap, and strive to live the rest of my life with excellence, I know he is pleased.

Ingredients of Worship

Our worship of God, like David's, is grounded in our relationship with him and flows out of that relationship. It is also grounded in our understanding of what God has done for us. To truly worship God we must:

1. know God,
2. understand what he has done for us, and
3. be grateful for what he has done for us.

Worship requires both our heart and our mind. It does not require musicians, a worship team, words on a screen, or anything of the kind. In order for David to worship God with such exuberance as the ark was entering Jerusalem, David had to have a full understanding of what the ark meant in the history of his people (his mind), as well as a deep appreciation of and gratitude for the work God had done through the ark (his heart). In order for any one of us to truly worship God today, we must understand the significance of what Jesus did on the cross (mind) and have claimed Jesus's work on the cross as a personal gift, gratefully entering into a relationship with him (heart). It doesn't end there, though. One must also be an active participant in that relationship, relating to God day in and day out, understanding that God is alive and well, and aware of how God is actively at work in each of our lives today.

Definitions of worship

Just as each person's relationship with God is individualized, each person's worship of God is also individualized and is not limited to how one behaves in a church service. Worship is far more than that. Worship is a lifestyle. "So whether you eat or drink, or whatever you do, do it all for the glory of God" (1 Corinthians 10:31).

In *The Purpose Driven Life* Rick Warren states, "Anything you do that brings pleasure to God is an act of worship."[8] He expands on this definition of worship in the foreword to *The Worship Answer Book* by Rick Muchow: "A simple definition of worship, based on the Great Commandment: Worship is any expression of our love to God—for who he is, what he has said, and what he's doing."[9] Joyce Meyer's definition of worship is as follows: "Worship is born in our hearts; it fills our thoughts and it is expressed through our mouths and through our bodies."[10]

She goes on to say that

> When we read about worship in the Bible, we are reading about a personal relationship, about spiritual intimacy, and about passionate expressions of devotion from people who love and worship God with all of their hearts. This is true worship—the kind that bubbles up out of us when we have the fire of God in our lives, when our love for Him spills out all over everything, and when we are zealous and enthusiastic about our dynamic relationship with Him.[11]

When you think about worship this way it becomes obvious that our whole life, not just our behavior in a church service, can be lived as an act of worship.

Chapter Seven

DISCIPLES

Once an individual accepts God's invitation for relationship and becomes part of his family, that individual needs to decide whether he or she would like to become a disciple of Jesus. As with any relationship, there are varying degrees of closeness and commitment that are possible. We can be as close to God or as distant from him as we choose to be—casual acquaintance, friend, best friend, or disciple.

What is a disciple?

A disciple is one who is taught. Marcus J. Borg, in his book *Jesus: A New Vision*, discusses what it means to be a disciple of Jesus Christ. Borg states, "To be a disciple of Jesus meant something more than being a student of a teacher. To be a disciple meant 'to follow after.' 'Whoever would be my disciple.' Jesus said, 'Let him follow me.' What does it mean to be a follower of Jesus? It means to take seriously what he took seriously, to be like him in some sense."[12]

The first disciples

Peter and Andrew were among the first, if not *the* first, disciples of Jesus and, as we know, both later became apostles. As we also know, Peter was hugely instrumental in establishing Jesus's church on earth.

There are varying accounts of how Peter became a disciple of Jesus. Mark's and Matthew's accounts are virtually identical. "One day as Jesus was walking along the shore of the Sea of Galilee, he saw two brothers–Simon, also called Peter, and Andrew–throwing a net into the water, for they fished for a living. Jesus called out to them, 'Come, follow me, and I will show you how to fish for people!' And they left their nets at once and followed him" (Matthew 4:18-20). Luke recounts the same incident, however, he expands the story including much more detail.

> One day as Jesus was preaching on the shore of the Sea of Galilee, great crowds pressed in on him to listen to the word of God. He noticed two empty boats at the water's edge, for the fishermen had left them and were washing their nets. Stepping into one of the boats, Jesus asked Simon, its owner, to push it out into the water. So he sat in the boat and taught the crowds from there.

> When he had finished speaking, he said to Simon, "Now go out where it is deeper, and let down your nets to catch some fish."

> "Master," Simon replied, "we worked hard all last night and didn't catch a thing. But if you say

so, I'll let the nets down again." And this time their nets were so full of fish they began to tear! A shout for help brought their partners in the other boat, and soon both boats were filled with fish and on the verge of sinking.

When Simon Peter realized what had happened, he fell to his knees before Jesus and said, "Oh Lord, please leave us—I'm such a sinful man." For he was awestruck by the number of fish they had caught, as were the others with him. His partners, James and John, the sons of Zebedee, were also amazed.

Jesus replied to Simon, "Don't be afraid! From now on you'll be fishing for people!" And as soon as they landed, they left everything and followed Jesus. Luke 5:1-11

Mark's and Matthew's accounts of the story are a bit hard for me to swallow. I would not drop everything and follow a complete stranger simply because he or she told me to. I don't know many people who would do that. Luke's account of the story makes it more believable. I imagine Peter must have been impressed or touched by Jesus's teaching, which was why he called him "Master" and took his boat out again on Jesus's "say so." When their nets became filled to overflowing with fish, Peter "realized what had happened" and reacted with humility. Peter seems to have known that Jesus was someone special and extraordinary and chose to walk away from his life and follow him.

However it happened that Jesus called Peter to follow him, Jesus undoubtedly called Peter to be his follower and Peter chose to do so. The same is true for everyone else who chooses to follow Jesus. It doesn't matter *how* we're called, it matters *that* we're called, and that we said *Yes*!

Followers of Jesus

The point was made previously that when Jesus walked the earth in the flesh, he consistently taught that love is more important than the law. He also consistently manifested compassion for anyone who was hurting or struggling. Therefore, it seems blatantly clear to me that Jesus took loving people seriously. During the last meal he shared with the apostles before he died, he told them, "I am giving you a new commandment: Love each other. Just as I have loved you, you should love each other. Your love for one another will prove to the world that you are my disciples" (John 13:34–35).

That command was not only for the apostles who knew Jesus in the flesh; it was and is for all his disciples throughout time. The love that followers of Jesus are called to exhibit, though, is not a worldly love. It is a Calvary-type love. What is a Calvary-type love? *Love* when considered this way is a verb. It is a choice. It is selfless. It is choosing to do something for someone else regardless of the cost to self. It is not a feeling. It is an action. It is Jesus carrying his cross to Calvary in Jerusalem and allowing Roman soldiers to nail him to it, and then staying nailed to it until he died.

Calvary-type love

Gregory Boyd, in his book *Repenting of Religion*, provides a description of Calvary-type love:

> While nonbelievers can be expected to love those who love them, disciples are called and empowered to love even their enemies and pray for those who persecute them. While nonbelievers can be expected to do good to those who do good to them, disciples are called and empowered to do good even to those who harm them . . . Our love must be given without consideration to the relative merits or faults of the person we encounter . . . We are to love without strings attached, without conditions, without any consideration whatsoever of the apparent worthiness of the person we encounter.[13]

Bruxy Cavey, in his book *The End of Religion*, provides another description of Calvary-type love:

> The way of Jesus is the way of risky love. Religion is the way of safety, security and shelter within the structure of rules, regulations, rituals, and routines. Jesus and his earliest followers were relentless in pressing people to see two things. First, loving people is the primary way we love God. Second, this love of humankind must always take precedence over religious ritual or ethnic obstacles . . . Christ-followers are called to be, according to the standards of this world,

"foolish." Real love is, from a purely human, self-serving perspective, irrational . . . Religious traditions can be a trap that keeps us from moving into unchartered territories of bold love and radical compassion. Irreligious people, on the other hand, are free to be more loving. Jesus calls people to love in such a way that all social barricades are broken, penetrated, subverted— including and especially those erected by religion. And to love like God wants, we must be willing to put practical service ahead of safety, comfort and convenience.[14]

Needless to say, loving others with a Calvary-type love is far from easy. So, what does it take to love like this? It takes first allowing oneself to be loved unconditionally. It is through the experience of being loved that one develops a healthy self-love. If you don't have love for self, you can't give love to others. Jesus himself made this point when he answered a question posed to him by a teacher of religious law: "'Which is the most important command in the laws of Moses?' Jesus replied, 'Love the Lord your God with all your heart, soul, and mind. This is the first and greatest commandment. The second most important is similar: Love your neighbor as much as you love yourself'" (Matthew 22:36–39 TLB). The operative words here are "as much as you love yourself." Again, if you don't have love for self, you can't give love to others. You can't give away what you don't have.

Bruxy Cavey put it this way: "Real Christ-followers are those who, having been on the receiving end of God's gracious love through Jesus, pour out this same embracing love to others in ways that mend broken relationships, heal inner wounds, and offer practical care for the helpless and hurting."[15]

Keeping oneself fueled

In order to consistently love with a Calvary-type love, one needs to be running on a full tank. Running on empty won't cut it. Refueling happens through the sun and water of our relationship with God—prayer and worship.

When I think about a follower of Jesus Christ, the image that comes to my mind is someone who has a retractable roof on the top of their head. Through prayer and worship that roof can be opened at any time, and life-giving, unconditional love and grace and power can flow through them, filling every nook, cranny, and crevice of their being. Once full, their arms stretch out in front of them, and that same love and grace and power flow out of each of their ten fingers to anyone and everyone they come in contact with. Sounds wonderful, doesn't it? I can assure you from personal experience that it is wonderful. Allowing oneself to be loved by God and then allowing oneself to be used by God to love others is one of the payoffs of becoming a disciple.

Something else

In addition to commanding us to love one another, Jesus told us what else we need to do if we wish to be his disciple: "If you do not carry your own cross and follow me, you cannot be my disciple" (Luke 14:27).

Carrying your cross means fulfilling the purpose God chose especially for you. Jesus came to earth to die on a cross. That was his purpose. God also put each of us on earth to fulfill a specific purpose that he chose for us and designed us to fulfill.

Contrary to popular opinion, carrying our cross does not result in pain and suffering. Rather, when we carry our own cross, we become who God created us to be. We are then filled with a peace and joy that cannot be attained through human effort. It can come only from God.

Finding the cross that had my name on it was not quick or easy. Carrying the cross was even harder, though the difficulties and pain of carrying the cross were balanced by a deep feeling of certainty (I knew that I knew that I knew) that I was exactly where I was supposed to be, doing exactly what I was created to do. The peace that accompanied this was the peace that surpasses human understanding, the peace that can come only from God. Nothing else can compare to the peace and the joy you experience when you are walking in the will of God for your life, when you know you are right where you are supposed to be, doing exactly what you were created to do, fulfilling God's purpose for your life. This is another payoff of choosing to become a disciple of Jesus.

Everyone has a purpose
If you are not sure whether you believe that God has a specific purpose for you, consider that the concept of God having a plan and a purpose for every individual he creates is referenced throughout the Bible.

Isaiah told Cyrus, a pagan king, that God wanted him to facilitate the release of the people of Judah from exile in Babylon so they could return to Jerusalem and rebuild the temple. When the people questioned God for working through a pagan king, Isaiah told them,

> "What sorrow awaits those who argue with their Creator.
>   Does a clay pot argue with its maker?
> Does the clay dispute with the one who shapes it, saying,
>   'Stop, you are doing it wrong!'
> Does the pot exclaim,
>   'How clumsy can you be!'
> How terrible it would be if a newborn baby
>   said to its father,
>   'Why was I born?
> or if it said to its mother,
>   'Why did you make me this way?'"

> This is what the Lord says –
>   the Holy One of Israel and your Creator:
> 'Do you question what I do for my children?
>   Do you give me orders about the work of my hands?
> I am the one who made the earth
>   and created people to live on it.
> With my hands I stretched out the heavens.
>   All the stars are at my command.
> I will raise up Cyrus to fulfill my righteous purpose,
>   and I will guide his actions.'"
> Isaiah 45:9–13

Isaiah was telling the people of Israel in no uncertain terms that God is sovereign, that he knows what he is doing, and that he chooses whomever he wants to do whatever he wants them to do.

Jeremiah also believed that God has a purpose and plan for everyone he creates. Jeremiah relayed this truth in a letter to the Israelites when they were in exile: "'For I know the plans I have for you,' says the LORD. 'They are plans for good and not for disaster, to give you a future and a hope'" (Jeremiah 29:11).

A New Testament figure who believed that God has a specific purpose for each individual he creates, and who had a very clear understanding and acceptance of the role God wanted him to play, was John the Baptist.

> At this time John the Baptist was baptizing at Aenon, near Salim . . . John's disciples came to him and said, "Rabbi, the man you met on the other side of the Jordan River, the one you identified as the Messiah, is also baptizing people. And everybody is going to him instead of coming here to us."
>
> John replied, "No one can receive anything unless God gives it from heaven. You yourselves know how plainly I told you, 'I am not the Messiah. I am only here to prepare the way for Him.'"
> John 3:23–28

The apostle Paul also believed this. In his letter to the church at Corinth Paul stated, "But we will not boast of authority we do not have. Our goal is to measure up to God's plan for us" (2 Corinthians 10:13 TLB).

Discovering your purpose

If you wish to discover the purpose for which God created you and you don't know how, here are some suggestions:

In *The Purpose Driven Life* Rick Warren gives the following suggestion as to how you might arrive at an understanding of God's purpose for your life:

> Before God created you, he decided what role he wanted you to play on earth. He planned exactly how he wanted you to serve him, and then he shaped you for those tasks. You are the way you are because you were made for a specific ministry . . . God never wastes anything. He would not give you abilities, interests, talents, gifts, personality, and life experiences unless he intended to use them for his glory. By identifying and understanding these factors, you can discover God's will for your life.[16]

John Maxwell, in *Becoming a Person of Influence*, puts it this way:

> God has created every person with a purpose. But not everyone discovers what that purpose is. To find out, get to know yourself—your strengths and weaknesses. Look at your opportunities. Examine where God has put you. Then seek His counsel. He will give you a vision for your life.[17]

The apostle Paul told the church in Rome, and us, that if we want to understand the purpose for which God created us, we need to detach from the ways of the world and learn God's ways: "Don't copy the behavior and customs of this world, but let God transform you into a new person by changing the way you think. Then you will learn to know God's will for you, which is good and pleasing and perfect" (Romans 12:2).

God's ways in no way, shape, or form match the ways of the world. As a matter of fact, God's standards and expectations contradict and challenge the commonly accepted values and standards of the world. They turn the world's standards upside down and inside out. The world says to take revenge on those who do us wrong; Jesus said to forgive them and be kind to them. The world says to hate our enemies; Jesus said to love them and pray for them. The world says to let people know the good things we've done so they will admire us; Jesus said to keep those good things secret. The world says to accumulate as much wealth and possessions as possible and hold onto them; Jesus said to give them away.

Therefore, anyone who is truly living his or her life according to God's ways can't help but stand out to others as belonging to God. Just as God wanted the ancient Israelites to live by a higher standard than their neighbors so their neighbors would know that they were his people, he wants twenty-first-century Christians to do the same for the same reason.

As with anything else, though, there are costs as well as payoffs for choosing to be a disciple of Jesus.

Cost of discipleship

In 2003 God revealed to me the purpose for which he had created me. As I lived out that purpose, I encountered much opposition. Most of the opposition I encountered, similar to what Jesus and his disciples and apostles encountered, came from religious people.

I was episodically lied about, betrayed, ostracized, abandoned, and had coup attempts (some successful, some not) organized against me. All of these were orchestrated by religious people. Some were orchestrated by religious leaders.

Though these episodes were painful and lonely to live through, they did not cause me to doubt the call God had placed on my life, nor did the pain outweigh the internal joy and sense of fulfillment I was experiencing as I walked in God's purpose for my life. In spite of this, though, I still needed to cope with the pain and loneliness. I coped with it by drawing strength and comfort from the following words of Jesus in the Sermon on the Mount:

> God blesses you when people mock you and persecute you and lie about you and say all sorts of evil things against you because you are my followers. Be happy about it! Be very glad! For a great reward awaits you in heaven. And remember, the ancient prophets were persecuted in the same way. Matthew 5:11–12

I know that I am far from the only person who has had to pay a price for choosing to be a disciple of Jesus. I also know that the price I have paid is very small in comparison to the price others have paid. After all, I'm still breathing.

Important decisions

The most important decision anyone will ever make, I believe, is whether or not to be a child of God, a member of God's family. This decision not only determines where one will spend eternity; it also determines the quality of one's life while on earth. Make no mistake, this decision needs to be conscious and intentional. To not decide is, in essence, to keep yourself apart from God's family.

The second most important decision one will ever make, I believe, is deciding which church body to be part of. If one decides to become a child of God, the church where one plants oneself is a critical determining factor in how one will grow as a Christian. I encourage you to also make this decision a conscious and intentional one—i.e., don't base your decision on location or on what denomination you grew up in, if you indeed grew up in a church. I encourage you to look carefully at a prospective church body to see if it is a church who truly follows Christ—that is, a new covenant church.

Personal Note: When I first started to travel in church circles as an adult, it never entered my mind that I needed to think about whether the church I was attending was a new covenant church and whether the leaders were committed to serving God or to fulfilling personal agendas. I naively assumed that church bodies and church leaders were committed to serving God and operated with integrity. This false assumption led to my being deeply wounded by church leaders when I tried to grow into the person God had created me to be and to fulfill the purpose he had chosen for me and designed me to fulfill.

Chapter Eight

NEW COVENANT CHURCHES

New covenant churches believe in and follow the teachings of Jesus (salvation by faith). Old covenant churches believe in and follow the Law of Moses (salvation by works). New covenant churches teach relationship. Old covenant churches teach religion. New covenant churches focus on the heart. Old covenant churches focus on behavior. New covenant churches are inclusive. Old covenant churches are exclusive.

Heart vs. behavior

God is a God of hearts. He is not nearly as interested in what we do as in why we do it. God doesn't want us to give him our behavior; he wants us to give him our hearts. "Turn your hearts to the LORD, the God of Israel" (Joshua 24:23). God is not interested in right behavior if it is fueled by wrong motives; remember that right behavior flows from a right heart, not vice versa. "A good person produces good things from the treasury of a good heart, and an evil person produces evil things from the treasury of an evil heart" (Matthew 12:35).

New covenant churches focus on the heart and trust that godly behavior will result once an individual's heart is fully devoted to God.

Inclusive versus exclusive

Bruxy Cavey discusses the inclusive/exclusive dynamic in his book *The End of Religion*:

> When faith becomes religion, people on the inside of the group begin to focus their attention on the perimeter, patrolling the boundaries to regulate who is in and who is out. They develop visible boundary markers, demarcations of holiness, which become important signs of group identity ... Groups that focus on their center may have less clear perimeters. But they will not be threatened by this perimeter ambiguity, because they are clear about the core of their identity. This, in turn, leads to greater compassion and acceptance ... Jesus-followers will not try to separate who is "saved" and who is not, who is in and who is out. Policing the perimeter is what religious people do, but not Christ-followers—at least, not Christ-followers who really want to follow Jesus.[18]

To illustrate the difference between an old covenant church and a new covenant church, take a look at an event that occurred during Jesus's earthly ministry:

One Sabbath day as Jesus was teaching in a synagogue, he saw a woman who had been crippled by an evil spirit. She had been bent double for eighteen years and was unable to stand up straight. When Jesus saw her, he called her over and said, "Dear woman, you are healed of your sickness!" Then he touched her, and instantly she could stand straight. How she praised God!

But the leader in charge of the synagogue was indignant that Jesus had healed her on the Sabbath day. "There are six days of the week for working," he said to the crowd. "Come on those days to be healed, not on the Sabbath."

But the Lord replied, "You hypocrites! Each of you works on the Sabbath day! Don't you untie your ox or your donkey from its stall on the Sabbath and lead it out for water? This dear woman, a daughter of Abraham, has been held in bondage by Satan for eighteen years. Isn't it right that she be released, even on the Sabbath?" Luke 13:10–16

If this were to happen in today's world, an old covenant church would be upset that the rules had been broken. A new covenant church would celebrate the healing.

The church's purpose

Jesus meant for the church to be his hands, feet, and heart in the world—that is, to function as his body after his physical body had died. He intended for the church to continue ministering to people as he had. Since healing and teaching were the two primary aspects of Jesus's earthly ministry, it would seem to logically follow that the two primary functions of a church should be the same—healing and teaching.

Healing ministry

I can't imagine I will get much of an argument from anyone when I say that the world is full of hurting, broken people who are struggling with anxiety, depression, anger management, addictions to all kinds of substances and behaviors, and on and on and on. Though there are many services and programs that help with all these struggles, many deal only with the visible manifestations of these problems. The roots of the problems, the reasons the struggles exist in the first place, are often overlooked. It has been my experience that, though therapy and recovery are immensely helpful in healing these problems and struggles, neither takes you the distance. The only thing that can truly heal the roots of the problems individuals struggle with is Jesus's love.

Broken, hurting, struggling people sought out Jesus. The Bible is full of stories of people who flocked to him, followed him, chased him down, overcame obstacles to get to him. Why? They knew he loved them, they knew he could heal them, and they felt safe enough to go to him. As members of his body, the church, we need to be conveying the same love, hope, and safety through creating an environment that is devoid of judgment.

Gregory Boyd puts it this way: "The community in which performance and hiding have ceased is a community in which healing can occur . . . Emotional wounds that are concealed are wounds that can never be healed. Only when people feel safe enough to reveal their innermost pain are they able to begin to deal with it, but this sort of safety requires a context that is free of judgment."[19]

Teaching ministry

The authors of *Breaking the Bondage of Legalism* state, "Millions of Americans who truly are Christian have failed to fully comprehend the gospel. It is as if they have one foot in the new covenant and another in the old."[20] When this happens, when regular churchgoers do not have a clear understanding of the true gospel, it breaks my heart, and I hold the leaders and teachers of their churches accountable for this. I believe that if regular churchgoers do not understand the gospel, it is most probably because they are not being taught the true gospel. The gospel is not complicated. It can be boiled down to:

1. Salvation is through faith in Jesus Christ. Period. There is nothing we can do to earn salvation.

2. When we accept Jesus's work on the cross as a personal gift, repent of our wrongdoings, and give our lives to him, we come into relationship with God, becoming part of his family.

3. The Holy Spirit then takes up residence inside us and slowly but surely transforms us from the inside out until we become like Jesus.

If churches are not teaching this, they are not new covenant churches. If you are not hearing week in and week out how to become part of God's family, how to nurture your relationship with God, how to hear from him, and how to become more like Jesus, you will have an uphill struggle to become who God wants you to be, and you may never experience the freedom that is available to you in Christ. I agree wholeheartedly with Bruxy Cavey when he says, "The real problem Christians need to face is not the exaggerated criticism of secular people, but the mind-blowing extent of the church's failure to follow Jesus."[21]

Churches as disciples

I believe that, just as God has a unique purpose for each individual he creates, he also has a unique purpose for each church body he gives birth to. Henry and Richard Blackaby echo this belief in their book *Spiritual Leadership*. They state, "God equips each church for particular assignments."[22] Before a congregation can understand and fulfill its particular assignment, however, it first needs to become, corporately, a genuine disciple of Jesus Christ.

Just as individuals who choose to follow Jesus are called to love with a Calvary-type love, churches that are truly following Jesus (new covenant churches) are also called to love with a Calvary-type love. How can you tell if a church is truly manifesting Calvary-type love? "When sinful, broken, hurting people are pleasantly surprised at how accepting we are, and religious people are outraged at how accepting we are, there is a good chance we're starting to live like Jesus."[23]

Important Note: Acceptance is not the same as agreement. We can accept people for who they are and love them for who they are without agreeing with or condoning what they do. We are called to love, not to judge. Jesus told us this in his Sermon on the Mount: "Do not judge others, and you will not be judged" (Matthew 7:1).

Gregory Boyd states:

All are supposed to see God as his love is displayed in the Body of Christ. Through the church, the world is supposed to literally witness and experience the perfect love that God eternally is. If the hearts of those in the world are at all open, they acknowledge the reality of the triune God because he is right there in front of them— in the loving community of the church! They witness firsthand the reality of Jesus because they encounter "his body."[24]

He goes on to say:

> The church as a whole has repeatedly failed to fulfill this mandate . . . We have tended to define ourselves as the promoter of good against evil and have often seen ourselves as specialists on good and evil. We have consequently become judges of good and evil rather than lovers of people regardless of whether they are good or evil.[25]

Not of this world

Just as Jesus's followers are to be in the world but not of the world, his church is to be in the world but not of the world. When Jesus stood before the Roman governor, Pontius Pilate, Pilate asked him, "Are you the king of the Jews?" (John 18:33). Jesus answered, "My Kingdom is not an earthly kingdom. . . . My Kingdom is not of this world" (John 18:36).

In his Sermon on the Mount Jesus told his followers to be light in a dark world. "'You are the light of the world—like a city on a hilltop that cannot be hidden. No one lights a lamp and then puts it under a basket. Instead, a lamp is placed on a stand, where it gives light to everyone in the house. In the same way, let your good deeds shine out for all to see, so that everyone will praise your heavenly Father'" (Matthew 5:14–16). I believe that Jesus wants the same thing from his church that he wants from his individual followers—i.e., to be light in a dark world. If his church is indeed to be light in a dark world, then the church most definitely needs to be so different from the world it is in that it stands out brightly and draws people to it.

The point was previously made that God's standards in no way, shape, or form match those of the world. A new covenant church, then, would be one that operates according to standards that in no way match those of the world. This church would not gauge its success or failure by the standards of the world (money, numbers, size). Rather, the measuring stick of success or failure for this church would be God's standard. What is God's standard? What does God want from us? As stated previously, God wants us to love people, to obey him, and to fulfill the purpose for which we were created. It would seem to logically follow, then, that in order for a particular church body to be successful in God's eyes it needs to do the same.

The stakes are high

"Without churches so filled with the power of God that they can't help but spill goodness and peace and love and joy into the world, depravity will win the day; evil will flood the world. But it doesn't have to be that way. Strong, growing communities of faith can turn the tide of history."[26]

In my opinion "strong, growing communities of faith" are new covenant churches who fully embrace and live out "the great irony."

> So here is the great irony—Jesus is happy to see his followers get organized in order to help spread the message that organizations are not the answer. Christ-followers read the Bible to learn of Jesus' teaching that reading the Bible is not what makes us a Christian. We pray regularly in

order to commune with the God who reminds us that praying regularly is not what makes us acceptable to him. We meditate to immerse our souls in the love of God that is already ours, not in order to somehow achieve a state of self-induced enlightenment. And we go to church to collectively celebrate the message that going to church is not what makes us God's children.[27]

Chapter Nine

GOD SENDS A HELPER

Early in his ministry Jesus spelled out God's expectations for every conceivable part of our lives in his most famous sermon, the Sermon on the Mount. (See Appendix Two.) As you read and ponder these expectations and consider the lifestyle Jesus modeled and calls us to live, it becomes clear just how different God's standards are from the standards of the world.

Toward the end of the Sermon on the Mount, Jesus acknowledged that the lifestyle he asks people to live is difficult. "You can enter God's Kingdom only through the narrow gate. The highway to hell is broad, and its gate is wide for the many who choose that way. But the gateway to life is very narrow and the road is difficult, and only a few ever find it" (Matthew 7:13–14).

The Israelites of the Old Testament showed us repeatedly and convincingly just how difficult it is to consistently live by God's standard. It's no easier today. What makes it so hard is that we're broken. All of us, every single one of us, are broken. We're broken in different ways and to different degrees—however, still broken.

If you're having a hard time wrapping your mind around the concept that you're broken, answer one or more of the following questions:

1. Have you ever done something you didn't want to do or didn't do something you wanted to do?
2. Have you ever said yes when you wanted to say no or said no when you wanted to say yes?
3. Have you been unable to break a habit that you know isn't good for you?
4. Have you repeated the same pattern of behavior over and over again in spite of numerous efforts to change it?
5. Do you have difficulty setting and/or sticking to limits re: eating, drinking, working, and so forth?
6. Do you feel you have to be doing something all the time, finding it almost intolerable to do nothing and just chill?

Each of these is an indicator of brokenness. Make of this what you will.

Paul's brokenness

The apostle Paul described his brokenness in his letter to the church in Rome.

So the trouble is not with the law, for it is spiritual and good. The trouble is with me, for I am all too human, a slave to sin. I don't really understand myself, for I want to do what is right, but I don't do it. Instead, I do what I hate. But if I know that what I am doing is wrong, this shows that I agree that the law is good. So I am not the one doing wrong; it is sin living in me that does it.

And I know that nothing good lives in me, that is, in my sinful nature. I want to do what is right, but I can't. I want to do what is good, but I don't. I don't want to do what is wrong, but I do it anyway. But if I do what I don't want to do, I am not really the one doing wrong; it is sin living in me that does it.

I have discovered this principle of life—that when I want to do what is right, I inevitably do what is wrong. I love God's law with all my heart. But there is another power within me that is at war with my mind. This power makes me a slave to the sin that is still within me. Oh, what a miserable person I am! Who will free me from this life that is dominated by sin and death? Thank God! The answer is in Jesus Christ our Lord. So you see how it is: In my mind I really want to obey God's law, but because of my sinful nature I am a slave to sin. Romans 7:14–25

Paul then went on to share God's solution to our brokenness.

The law of Moses was unable to save us because of the weakness of our sinful nature. So God did what the law could not do. He sent his own Son in a body like the bodies we sinners have. And in that body God declared an end to sin's control over us by giving his Son as a sacrifice for our sins. He did this so that the just requirement of the law would be fully satisfied for us, who no longer follow our sinful nature but instead follow the Spirit. Romans 8:3–4

John Fischer's explanation of this is in chapter four. As it is pertinent to this discussion, I am going to share it again here:

The Old Covenant requires a standard of performance and a reason to be obedient to it. But the standard, in its truest form, is impossible to pull off consistently. It could be argued that this is the whole point of God's dealings with humanity through the covenants. The Old Covenant is there to break us, to show us that we cannot live according to its precepts—that sin and selfishness dwell in us to a significant degree so as to rule out the possibility of following even the clear call of Jesus to love God, self, and others. This inability to follow the standard, along with its accompanying humility, qualifies us for a Savior—someone who will fulfill the law on our behalf and grant us righteousness as a free gift.

This is God's grace as given to us in the New Covenant through the death and resurrection of our Lord and Savior Jesus Christ.[28]

God's solution

God knew that, because of our brokenness, we would be unable on our own to consistently live by the Ten Commandments he gave Moses and the lifestyle Jesus laid out in the Sermon on the Mount, so he sent us a helper. That helper is the Holy Spirit. When we give our life to Jesus, God's Spirit, the Holy Spirit, comes to live inside us. If we cooperate with him, he will heal our brokenness.

During his time on earth, Jesus talked to his disciples about the Holy Spirit. When Jesus sent the apostles on their first mission trip, he told them about the role the Holy Spirit would play in their lives and in their ministries.

You will stand trial before governors and kings because you are my followers. But this will be your opportunity to tell the rulers and other unbelievers about me. When you are arrested, don't worry about how to respond or what to say. God will give you the right words at the right time. For it is not you who will be speaking—it will be the Spirit of your Father speaking through you. Matthew 10:18–20

At the last meal he shared with the apostles prior to his death, Jesus again spoke to them about the Holy Spirit.

"If you love me, obey my commandments. And I will ask the Father, and he will give you another Advocate, one who will never leave you. He is the Holy Spirit, who leads into all truth. The world cannot receive him, because it isn't looking for him and doesn't recognize him. But you know him, because he lives with you now and later will be in you." John 14:15–17

During the times that Jesus appeared to his disciples following his crucifixion and resurrection from the dead, he continued to talk to them about the Holy Spirit. "Once when he was eating with them, he commanded them, 'Do not leave Jerusalem until the Father sends you the gift he promised, as I told you before. John baptized with water, but in just a few days you will be baptized with the Holy Spirit'" (Acts 1:4–5).

At the end of forty days, Jesus ascended into heaven. Prior to his ascension, he told his disciples, "You will receive power when the Holy Spirit comes upon you. And you will be my witnesses, telling people about me everywhere—in Jerusalem, throughout Judea, in Samaria, and to the ends of the earth" (Acts 1:8). As Jesus promised, the Holy Spirit came to the disciples soon after Jesus ascended into heaven.

On the day of Pentecost all the believers were meeting together in one place. Suddenly, there was a sound from heaven like the roar of a mighty windstorm, and it filled the house where they were sitting. Then, what looked like flames or tongues of fire appeared and settled on each of them. And everyone present was filled with the Holy Spirit and began speaking in other languages, as the Holy Spirit gave them this ability. Acts 2:1–4

Filled with the power of the Holy Spirit, Peter then went outside and spoke to the crowd gathered there. Among other things, he told them that the gift of the Holy Spirit is promised to everyone who becomes a follower of Jesus. He said,

> "Each of you must repent of your sins and turn to God, and be baptized in the name of Jesus Christ for the forgiveness of your sins. Then you will receive the gift of the Holy Spirit. This promise is to you, and to your children, and even to the Gentiles—all who have been called by the Lord our God." Acts 2:38–39

When the Holy Spirit takes up residence inside us, he instills in us the fruit of the Spirit and gives us our spiritual gifts.

Paul described the fruit of the Spirit in his letter to the church in Galatia. "The Holy Spirit produces this kind of fruit in our lives: love, joy, peace, patience, kindness, goodness, faithfulness, gentleness, and self-control" (Galatians 5:22–23). If we cooperate with the Holy Spirit, he will grow these fruits in us to make us more Christlike.

Important Note: It is important to remember that our ungodly thoughts and behaviors do not immediately go away when we become part of God's family. They are slowly transformed into godly thoughts and behaviors as we cooperate with the Holy Spirit. You may believe that you need only to accept Christ as your Lord and Savior for your life to be complete and satisfying. The proclamation that "I am a born-again Christian, my past is washed clean, I am a new creature, and Christ has totally changed me" is true. Our spirits are born again. Our flesh, however, is holding on to a lifetime of hurts and destructive habits (our brokenness). The likelihood that you have no behaviors, thoughts, or attitudes that need to be changed and/or wounds that need to be healed is nonexistent. I believe that it is impossible for anyone to grow to adulthood without accruing some hurts along the way and developing some destructive habits or hang-ups.

Paul discussed spiritual gifts in his letter to the church in Corinth and his letter to the church in Rome:

> A spiritual gift is given to each of us so we can help each other. To one person the Spirit gives the ability to give wise advice; to another the same Spirit gives a message of special knowledge. The same Spirit gives great faith to another, and to someone else the one Spirit gives the gift of healing. He gives one person the power to perform miracles, and another the ability to prophesy. He gives someone else the ability to discern whether a message is from the Spirit

of God or from another spirit. Still another person is given the ability to speak in unknown languages, while another is given the ability to interpret what is being said. It is the one and only Spirit who distributes all these gifts. He alone decides which gift each person should have. 1 Corinthians 12:7–11

In his grace, God has given us different gifts for doing certain things well. So if God has given you the ability to prophesy, speak out with as much faith as God has given you. If your gift is serving others, serve them well. If you are a teacher, teach well. If your gift is to encourage others, be encouraging. If it is giving, give generously. If God has given you leadership ability, take the responsibility seriously. And if you have a gift for showing kindness to others, do it gladly. Romans 12:6–8

Our spiritual gifts are given to us to equip us to fulfill our God-given purpose. So, identifying your spiritual gifts is another way for you to understand the purpose for which God created you. Numerous spiritual gift inventories are available to help you do just that.

Whether or not we choose to fulfill our God-appointed purpose—i.e., carry our cross—is up to us. It is our choice. As previously stated, when we carry our cross we become fully who God created us to be and experience an internal peace and joy that are beyond human understanding or attainment. It is something that can come only from God.

There is also another side to this whole concept of fulfilling God's purpose for our life. That is, we are not the only ones who lose when we fail to discover and fulfill our purpose. Due to the system of human interdependence that God designed, everything we do or fail to do affects others. By not discovering and fulfilling God's plan for us, we not only miss out on experiencing joy and peace, but others miss out as well. In *The Purpose Driven Life* Rick Warren states, "God designed each of us so there would be no duplication in the world. No one has the exact same mix of factors that make you unique. That means no one else on earth will ever be able to play the role God planned for you. If you don't make your unique contribution to the body of Christ, it won't be made."[29]

Chapter Ten

MY TRANSITION AND BEYOND

Accepting God's invitation for a personal relationship with him through his Son, Jesus Christ, was, for me, not quick or easy. It was a rather long process during which I had to come to terms with the reality that many of the things I had been taught about God as I was growing up were simply not true. I wrestled with beliefs that I had embraced unquestioningly as a child, and I struggled with decisions about whether to hold on to those beliefs or let go of them and embrace realities I was hearing about as an adult. I eventually decided in favor of new beliefs and began my walk with Jesus. This process took place in the mid- to late 1990s.

The beginning

I grew up as the oldest of four children in an Irish Catholic family in northeastern New Jersey, not far from New York City. My biological parents were together; we had food, clothing, and shelter; had strong ties to extended family; and went to church (Catholic) and school (Catholic). In addition, there was no physical or sexual abuse. In spite of all this, though, my family was still broken. It was broken because my parents were physically present but emotionally absent, resulting in emotional neglect and thus preventing an authentic connection or attachment.

For example, we tended to have very lively, and sometimes rather loud, discussions around the dinner table. The discussions, however, almost always revolved around politics, sports, and world events. Opinions were debated. Feelings were never shared. What went on inside each of us on an emotional, human level was never acknowledged or even mentioned. The result of this was that my feelings became like foreign objects to me. I was totally unaware of them, totally cut off from them.

Two lessons I learned growing up in my family (lessons that, of course, I didn't realize at the time I was learning them) were:

1. Other people's opinions were very important, and I needed to please others and gain people's approval.

2. I needed to earn self-worth and love through what I did. The idea that I could be loved and valued just for who I was, separate from what I did, was completely off my radar, totally outside my frame of reference. The paths to earning love, acceptance, worth, and value that I found, or that were laid out for me, were academic achievement and taking care of others in my family.

I subsequently grew into an approval seeker, people pleaser, and overachiever *par excellence!* I was filled with a drivenness to always "do," accompanied by chronic feelings of inadequacy. No matter what I did, how much I did, or how well I did it, it was never enough, or so I thought. The image I had in my mind of what I thought I should be, compared to my picture of what I thought I was, taunted me constantly. It was the fuel that powered my dysfunctional, performance-based patterns of overachieving and compulsive caretaking, as well as the anxiety that accompanied these behaviors. I was constantly worrying about whether I had done enough, and since my picture of "enough" was totally beyond what any human being could possibly do, there was no way I could win. Therefore, anxiety was my constant companion.

Parallel track

While I was learning at home that I had to earn my parents' love and acceptance by what I did, I was learning in church (Catholic) and in school (Catholic) that I also had to earn God's love and earn salvation. I learned that my salvation was dependent on what I did (good works), not on what Christ did for me. I learned a very complex system of checks and balances, in which certain types and amounts of good works and penance made up for certain sins, and sins were divided into categories of venial and mortal. I learned that if I died with mortal sins on my soul that I had not sufficiently made up for with good works and penance, I would spend time suffering in purgatory to purge my soul of these sins. The amount of time I would spend in purgatory would depend on where I was in this check-and-balance system regarding sins and good deeds at the time of my death. This greatly increased my anxiety and contributed significantly to my sense of not being able to measure up, no matter what I did. Due to this I was not only afraid of life on earth, I also afraid of life in the hereafter.

My picture of God was of a very cold, distant, critical deity who didn't care about how I felt or what I needed and who had very high expectations of me, so high it was impossible for me to ever reach them. To complicate the issue, I knew he wouldn't love me or welcome me home unless I achieved them. He certainly was not someone I could trust or depend on. He was someone to be afraid of and stay away from.

During my early adulthood I drifted away from church and away from God. I didn't miss anything in my life because church to me was performing empty rituals that I didn't understand and reciting memorized responses and prayers that I also didn't understand. To me, God was just one more person for whom, no matter what I did or how much I did, it would never be enough. I didn't go back to church until after I became a parent. It was my children who brought me back to church and eventually to God.

Back to church

It was important to me that my children develop good morals and values, and I figured that the best way to make this happen was to raise them in a church, though I knew I did not want to raise them in the Catholic Church. So, not long after my second child was born, I started to look around for a church to join. We eventually settled on a United Methodist church and started attending regularly.

At first I was going for the kids, though it wasn't long before I started going for myself. I started hearing things like Christ died for me and God wanted a personal relationship with me. Those were totally foreign concepts to me and very difficult to wrap my mind around. What really blew my mind, though, was when I learned in a Bible study that there was no such thing as purgatory. That was just too much, and that brought into question everything I had been taught growing up.

I then went through a period of questioning, searching, and deciding what I believed and what I didn't believe.

The questioning and searching brought me face-to-face with childhood doctrines I had been taught and had believed without question, causing a few head-on collisions with these doctrines. The process also brought me to some forks in the road where I needed to make decisions between old beliefs and new beliefs. The process went like this: my head would decide in favor of new beliefs, emotional turmoil would inevitably follow, and once the emotional turmoil was resolved my heart would catch up.

Two of the head-on collisions I encountered in my faith journey involved sin and grace.

Spiritual re-education

Fully grasping the seriousness of sin was very difficult for me. I just couldn't understand why Protestants were always talking about sin and putting so much more emphasis on it than Catholics did. I also had a hard time with the concept that all sin is equally grievous to God. A phrase I heard often that nearly drove me crazy was "sin is sin." I kept trying to put sin into a hierarchy of seriousness. Reading James McCarthy's book *The Gospel According to Rome* helped me immensely in understanding why this was such a difficult struggle for me. In his discussion of sin and the sacrament of penance, Mr. McCarthy asks, "What is the outcome when a sinner confesses a grievous sin to a priest and then is told that he can atone for the . . . sin by doing something as simple as saying a few Hail Marys and Our Fathers? The sinner can only conclude that sin is not very serious."[30]

This is exactly what I had concluded. McCarthy addressed this very issue and clarified my struggle by saying

> The Lord never distinguished between sins in terms of their ultimate penalty. Jesus taught that every sin warrants eternal punishment in hell . . . Roman Catholicism, on the other hand, teaches that some sins are "light sins," minor infractions of the moral laws of God . . . Small sins, venial sins, do not bring eternal punishment . . . The Church even says that if mitigating circumstances exist, not even the gravest sin merits eternal punishment. . . . Consequently, though the Bible teaches that all sins are mortal, the Church teaches that no sin is necessarily mortal. And, though the Bible never mentions venial sin, the Church teaches that every sin could potentially be venial![31]

Fully grasping the true nature of grace was equally difficult, if not more difficult, for me. Once again, James McCarthy provided me with a clear understanding of my struggle. In his discussion of salvation, McCarthy stated that "the Church distorted biblical grace beyond recognition."[32]

The essence of biblical grace is beautifully described by the apostle Paul in his letter to Titus, a pastor on the island of Crete. Paul wrote:

> When God our Savior revealed his kindness and love, he saved us, not because of the righteous things we had done, but because of his mercy. He washed away our sins, giving us a new birth and new life through the Holy Spirit. He generously poured out the Spirit upon us through Jesus Christ our Savior. Because of his grace he declared us righteous and gave us confidence that we will inherit eternal life. Titus 3:4–7

According to Paul, God's grace is characterized by kindness, love, and mercy. In addition, Paul made it explicitly clear that God bestows his grace on us because of what Jesus did, not because of anything we did and not because we deserve it.

The Roman Catholic Church, on the other hand, teaches, in McCarthy's words, that

> Sanctifying grace is a gift of the Holy Spirit initially given to individuals through the sacrament of baptism. It then "abides in them," making them continually holy and pleasing to God . . . The

Catholic is said to be in the state of grace. This is the customary or habitual state of his soul. For this reason, sanctifying grace is often called habitual grace ... A baptized Catholic can forfeit sanctifying grace in his soul through serious, conscious, and deliberate sin. Should this happen, the sacrament of penance can restore sanctifying grace ... Actual grace is a supernatural assistance to do good and avoid evil. Actual grace enlightens the mind and inspires the will to perform good works necessary for salvation. Unlike sanctifying grace, which has a constant influence upon the soul, actual grace is a temporary strengthening. It is the promise of God's helping hand in time of need. It is a momentary aid for a specific action, which passes with the using. Therefore, actual grace must be continually replenished. This is accomplished through the sacraments.[33]

The seven sacraments of the Catholic Church are Baptism, Penance, Eucharist, Confirmation, Matrimony, Holy Orders, and Anointing of the Sick. McCarthy continued his discussion of grace with:

The Church teaches that these seven sacraments are the primary means by which God bestows sanctifying and actual grace upon the faithful ... The sacraments are said to "contain" grace. They are not merely symbolic expressions of grace that God gives to those who believe. Rather, each sacrament is a channel of God's grace, the "instrumental cause" of grace. God is believed to confer grace upon Catholics by means of the sacraments through the proper performance of the sacramental ritual . . . The Roman Catholic Church teaches that the sacraments are necessary for salvation.[34]

The Catholic Church also teaches that an individual can earn an increase in sanctifying grace through the performance of good works. McCarthy concluded his discussion of grace by stating:

Not only did the Church obscure the meaning of grace, but it altered its very essence. Grace became the medium of exchange in the Church's merit system: Do work, earn grace. The more grace you have, the harder you work. The harder you work, the more grace you earn . . . Biblical grace cannot be dispensed like a product from a machine. Neither would the Father, having removed the barrier of sin at such a high cost, now place sacraments between Himself and His children. God wants His children dependent upon Him, not sacraments. He offers a relationship, not a ritual. Roman Catholic theology makes people dependent upon the sacraments for salvation and thereby dependent upon the Church . . . The belief that sacraments, and thereby the Roman Catholic Church itself, are necessary for salvation has no biblical support. The Scriptures say nothing about seven sacraments as the primary channels of God's grace. Neither do they speak of an institution such as the Roman Catholic Church as the administrator of the sacraments. The Bible teaches that God's grace is offered freely and directly to all who trust in Christ.[35]

The Catholic Church, therefore, is an old covenant church. They have not embraced the lesson of the veil tearing in two at the time of Jesus's death. They preach and practice that an individual needs a priest to act as an intermediary between himself/herself and God. The belief that an individual can have direct access to God without anyone else's help is totally outside their frame of reference.

My conclusions

I eventually came to the conclusion that the God of my childhood is not the real God. I began to believe that God really does love me and care about how I feel and what I need and that he will take care of me and provide for me. I developed that belief by spending months reading the following Scripture passage from the Sermon on the Mount every day:

That is why I tell you not to worry about everyday life—whether you have enough food and drink, or enough clothes to wear. Isn't life more than food, and your body more than clothing? Look at the birds. They don't plant or harvest or store food in barns, for your heavenly Father feeds them. And aren't you far more valuable to him than they are? Can all your worries add a single moment to your life?

And why worry about your clothing? Look at the lilies of the field and how they grow. They don't work or make their clothing, yet Solomon in all his glory was not dressed as beautifully as they are. And if God cares so wonderfully for wildflowers that are here today and thrown into the fire tomorrow, he will certainly care for you. Why do you have so little faith?

So don't worry about these things, saying, 'What will we eat? What will we drink? What will we wear?' These things dominate the thoughts of unbelievers, but your heavenly Father already knows all your needs. Seek the Kingdom of God above all else, and live righteously, and he will give you everything you need. Matthew 6:25–33

Along with developing the belief that God will take care of me, I began to understand that he wants to be involved in my life day to day, minute to minute (not just for an hour on Sunday morning) and that he loves me so much that he sent his only Son, Jesus, to suffer and die for me and that Jesus would have suffered and died even if I were the only person on the planet! I finally understood and believed that he wants me to have a relationship with Jesus and to follow Jesus, not a bunch of man-made rules like whether or not I eat meat on Friday. And I finally grasped that there was nothing I could do to earn salvation, that it was a gift freely offered that I could either choose to accept or not accept. I chose to accept it and started my walk with Jesus.

As I made the transition from religion to relationship, I gradually came to understand that God is a God of hearts. He is not nearly as interested in what I do as in why I do it. I realized that God didn't want me to give him my behavior; he wanted me to give him my heart. "'Turn your hearts to the LORD, the God of Israel'" (Joshua 24:23). I learned that he is not interested in right behavior if it is fueled by wrong motives and that right behavior flows from a right heart, not vice versa. "'A good person produces good things from the treasury of a good heart, and an evil person produces evil things from the treasury of an evil heart'" (Matthew 12:35).

As God performed surgery on my heart to align it with his values, I began to see that I needed to put him front and center in my life and make my relationship with him my top priority. That was the only way my heart would be right. As I did this, I came to understand that religion can be practiced in one's spare time; however, relationship requires total commitment. "Don't look for shortcuts to God. The market is flooded with surefire, easygoing formulas for a successful life that can be practiced in your spare time. Don't fall for that stuff, even though crowds of people do. The way to life—to God!—is vigorous and requires total attention" (Matthew 7:13–14 MSG).

Additional cost

As I put God front and center in my life, I paid another price for choosing to be a disciple of Jesus. That price was struggle and conflict in many of my human relationships. Friends, including church friends, and family members who had not taken the step to put God first in their lives did not understand what was going on with me and were threatened by the changes they saw in me. For my part, I became frustrated and uncomfortable with those who had not given their lives to God. The discrepancy between God's values and the values of the world became crystal clear to me. I no longer fit in with people who were living their lives according to the standards of the world. I truly began to feel that, though I was in the world, I was not of the world. I was comforted by the following words of Jesus to his disciples: "If the world hates you, remember that it hated me first. The world would love you as one of its own if you belonged to it. But you are no longer part of the world. I chose you to come out of the world, so it hates you" (John 15:18–19).

Tension and distance settled in to many of my human relationships, particularly my relationships with members of my family of origin. At first this really disturbed me, and I thought something was wrong. I then came across the following words of Jesus to his disciples: "Do you think I have come to bring peace to the earth? No, I have come to divide people against each other! From now on families will be split apart, three in favor of me, and two against—or two in favor and three against" (Luke 12:51–52). I then knew that all was as it should be.

Though I was reassured by these words of Jesus, the tension and conflict between me and members of my family of origin continued to distress me. At first, I didn't see how I was contributing to the tension and conflict. Gradually my eyes were opened, and I saw that I was not accepting them for who they were. I wanted them to make the same choices I had made, and I was angry at them for not making these choices. As I moved away from the anger and accepted them for who they were, the tension eased and the conflict decreased.

I don't want to mislead you by seeming to convey that this was quick and/or easy. It was neither. In reality it was, and continues to be, rather difficult. Though these relationships are far from conflict-free and tension-free, they are much healthier and more relaxed than in the past. For my part, I am continuing to work on accepting these family members for who they are and loving them unconditionally. In short, I am trying to be Jesus to them.

Finding my cross

Fairly early in my faith walk I started experiencing a nagging sense that I was supposed to do something for God. It kept gnawing at me inside and wouldn't go away. Though I had this feeling that I was supposed to do something for God, I didn't have the faintest idea what it was I was supposed to do. In an effort to understand what it was I was supposed to do, I served on and then led a committee in my church and also served in a number of different ministries. Though these were good and enjoyable and somewhat fulfilling, not one of them felt like the right fit.

This all changed in the fall of 2002 following a worship service in which the preacher spoke about being ashamed of our relationship with Jesus. He looked at the congregation and emphatically stated, "Never be ashamed of your relationship with Jesus Christ!" I felt as though he were speaking right to me. I knew I had been a closet Christian. I went right home and got down on my knees and apologized to God for being ashamed of my relationship with his Son. I immediately felt adrenaline surge throughout my whole body, and God, right then and there, gave me a directive regarding something he wanted me to do for him. He wanted me to lead a small group for converts from Catholicism. I did that. Then, in spring/early summer of 2003 a notice went out to all the small group leaders that the Senior Pastor was going to Saddleback Church in California to learn about a faith-based recovery program called Celebrate Recovery. The notice included an open invitation for anyone who was interested to join him. I went, and while I was there God finally let me know what he wanted me to do for him. He let me know beyond the shadow of a doubt that he wanted me to lead the Celebrate Recovery ministry my church was about to start. When we returned to our home church, we did start a Celebrate Recovery ministry, and I did become the ministry leader.

What followed was one of the most difficult years of my life. One would think that once I finally understood what God wanted me to do, all would be clear sailing, right? Wrong! Nothing could be further from the truth. Establishing and leading the Celebrate Recovery ministry was far harder than I had ever imagined it would be. It was full of struggle, challenges, conflict, anger, hurt, fear, and self-doubt. Power battles abounded. My leadership was constantly challenged and undermined.

There was a period of time in spring 2004 during which I was particularly discouraged and full of doubt. One morning while I was praying, I asked God to show me what I needed to read or to hear, and I opened my Bible. It opened to 1 Chronicles 28 (David commissioning Solomon to build the temple). I started to read that chapter, and the last two verses (20–21) almost jumped off the page at me: "Then David continued, 'Be strong and courageous and do the work. Don't be afraid or discouraged by the size of the task, for the LORD God, my God, is with you. He will not fail you or forsake you. He will see to it that all the work related to the Temple of the LORD is finished correctly. The various divisions of priests and Levites will serve in the Temple of God. Others with skills of every kind will volunteer, and the leaders and the entire nation are at your command.'"

This confirmed to me that God did indeed want me to be a leader. I began to read those verses every day, sometimes multiple times in one day, and I slowly began to feel the burden of weight lifted off my shoulders. I knew that I wasn't alone and that God was in control. I didn't have to be. All I had to do was follow his plan, and he would do the rest. As I trusted that more and more, my faith became stronger and my fear decreased. I stopped people pleasing and approval seeking, and I started to truly lead.

In August 2004 I went back to Saddleback Church for the 2004 Celebrate Recovery Summit. Being there I felt as though I were home. I knew I had finally found the exact right fit. When I returned to my home church and ministry from the 2004 Celebrate Recovery Summit, I began to lead with a greater degree of confidence and purpose. I knew I was walking in the will of God for my life. I knew who God had created me to be, and I not only felt good about it—I rejoiced in it. As I truly led the ministry, however, the challenges to my leadership and the power struggles intensified, until they culminated in a head-on collision with the stained-glass ceiling.

In November '04 I was removed from the position of Celebrate Recovery Ministry leader by the pastors and some other leaders in the church. I hadn't seen this coming and was initially in shock. When the shock lessened, I was devastated. I began a period of deep grieving and mourning. I was hurt, angry, and depressed. I felt as though I were wandering in the wilderness, lost.

I've heard it said that great lessons are learned in times of great pain, and that certainly proved to be true for me. It's difficult to describe the depth of joy I had felt at finally discovering and fulfilling God's purpose for my life. It's even more difficult to describe the depth of pain I felt at having that ripped away from me by human beings.

Although I was devastated and in more emotional pain than at almost any other time in my life, I never once doubted God's call on my life. I saw my removal from the leadership of Celebrate Recovery as a human thing and not a God thing. At the same time, I also believed that it could not have happened unless God had allowed it to happen.

During my time in the wilderness God brought me much closer to him, teaching me to trust him, his timing, and his plan on a much deeper level. He also taught me that my source of self-esteem and self-worth is not in my professional work or in my ministry, as I had previously thought. It's in my relationship with him—and I belong to him, not to any particular church or ministry. I know that I know that I know that he will not abandon me or forsake me, no matter what. I don't have to perform, achieve, take care of anyone, please others, or gain others' approval in order for God to love me. He loves me no matter what, and he knew me and loved me before he placed me in my mother's womb.

Though God taught me these invaluable lessons during my time in the wilderness, the most profound lesson he taught me was how to forgive. My healing process moved along in fits and starts. I experienced victories followed by relapses. As this happened repeatedly, I came to understand that God had a very special purpose for this time in my life.

I gradually began to understand that, just as he had given me the Celebrate Recovery ministry to lead in order to break my spirit of independence, he allowed it to be taken away from me in order to teach me how to forgive. He slowly and convincingly revealed to me my spirit of unforgiveness. I came to see that my life was not characterized by forgiveness, as Jesus wants his followers' lives to be. Rather, my life was characterized by holding grudges and harboring bitterness, resentment, and a desire for vengeance. Though I knew that forgiveness is at the heart of the gospel message and had received God's forgiveness for my sins when I accepted Jesus's work on the cross, I was not extending forgiveness to others who had wronged or hurt me. God showed me that I was not walking out this vital part of the Christian walk. He further showed me that my spirit of unforgiveness would stop me from fulfilling my destiny. As this realization took root in me, I began to study forgiveness. I came across a definition of forgiveness in Lewis B. Smedes's book *The Art of Forgiving*. That definition is this: "Forgiving . . . is an art, a practical art, maybe the most neglected of all the healing arts. It is the art of healing inner wounds inflicted by other people's wrongs."[36] As I continued to study forgiveness, I learned what forgiveness is—and what it is not.

I learned that forgiveness is:

- A choice: I don't have to feel like forgiving someone to forgive him or her
- A free gift given with no strings attached
- Surrendering our right to get even
- Choosing to keep no record of the wrongs
- Being merciful
- Being gracious
- Letting go of bitterness
- A heart condition: Forgiveness takes place in the forgiver's heart. It is intrapersonal, not interpersonal
- A permanent condition, a lifelong commitment: I cannot forgive someone and take it back later

I learned that forgiveness is not:

- Forgetting
- Excusing the wrong that was done
- Tolerating the wrong that was done
- Denying the wrong that was done
- Justifying what was done
- Pardoning what was done
- Refusing to take the wrong seriously
- Pretending that we are not hurt
- Erasing the need for consequences
- Quick
- Easy
- A magic balm that takes away feelings of hurt and anger

Though all of the above lessons I learned about forgiveness were important, the three most important ones were:

1. The choice to forgive does not depend on the wrongdoer's attitude or perception of the wrong. I can choose to forgive someone whether or not they see themselves as having done something wrong and whether or not they are sorry.

2. Forgiveness is not the same thing as reconciliation. I can forgive someone and choose not to re-enter a relationship with him/her.

3. Forgiveness is an essential, nonnegotiable ingredient in the healing of deep wounds. In these instances, forgiving benefits the forgiver far more than the forgiven.

As I struggled to forgive the pastors and other church leaders who had removed me from the position of Celebrate Recovery ministry leader, I fought against my desire to get back at them, to make them hurt as much as they had hurt me. During this process I was comforted by the following words of Lewis B. Smedes in *Forgive and Forget: Healing the Hurts We Don't Deserve*: "Nobody seems to be born with much talent for forgiving. We all need to learn from scratch, and the learning almost always runs against the grain."[37]

As I worked on forgiving those who had hurt me, I quickly realized that I could not do it on my own. My desire for vengeance was too strong. I needed God's help, his power. I began to daily ask God to give me an attitude and lifestyle of forgiveness. I simultaneously made a decision that I was no longer going to allow those pastors and leaders to steal my joy. They had already taken too much from me, and I was not going to allow them to take anything more. As I daily prayed this prayer and reiterated my decision, my peace and joy slowly came back, and I was finally able to exit the wilderness.

Moving on

I then served in a number of different capacities in various Celebrate Recovery ministries in my area. I eventually found my way to a Celebrate Recovery ministry at which I was asked to lead their team. In August 2009 I again attended the Celebrate Recovery Summit at Saddleback Church. The passion and commitment to Celebrate Recovery emanating from everyone there was the same as it had been five years earlier, and I experienced the same sense of belonging, of being home, that I had previously experienced. God confirmed to me loudly and clearly that he wanted me to be a Celebrate Recovery leader. So, I served as the leader of that Celebrate Recovery team for four years.

Those four years were also difficult. Though they were not marked by the same level of conflict, struggle, challenges, and power battles as the first Celebrate Recovery ministry, I did encounter opposition.

When 2013 began I started to reap what I had sown and harvest what I had planted. The consequences of a lifetime of failing to take care of my physical body caught up with me. Some medical problems I had been ignoring could no longer be ignored. I needed two major surgeries. I then stepped out of leadership of that Celebrate Recovery ministry and spent the following year taking care of my physical body. During that time I came to realize that my season of being a Celebrate Recovery leader was over. I then entered a period of waiting on God to let me know what he wanted me to do next—and he did.

In July 2014 God lit a fire in my heart to help his daughters be set free from belief systems and practices that reinforce the inequality of the sexes. In response to that fire being lit, I wrote *When the Glass Ceiling is Stained, Who's the Architect?* and later wrote *When Going with the Flow Isn't Enough, Swim Upstream.* I now swim upstream against gender inequality whenever and wherever I see it.

Final piece

A very important and difficult part of my spiritual journey has been coming to terms with my Catholic upbringing. The Catholic Church did not lead me to God. On the contrary, the Catholic Church erected many obstacles on the path to God—roadblocks that seemed impossible to overcome.

As I read and studied, I came to see how the Catholic Church took very simple concepts and complicated them to the point that it was next to impossible to understand them. The church instilled fear and apprehension in me and solidified the toxic shame that had developed as I grew up in my family. Rather than teaching me that God loved me, the Catholic Church taught me that I was not good enough for God and would never be good enough, no matter what I did. The whole concept of having a personal relationship with a loving God was totally absent. It was nowhere on my radar screen.

As the discrepancies between Roman Catholic doctrine and Scripture became clearer and clearer to me, I became very angry at the Catholic Church. I was angry at the church for teaching me and countless others a distorted gospel—a gospel that leads to fear, anxiety, and shame rather than peace, joy, and love. My anger at the Catholic Church simmered under the surface for years and would flare up whenever I would attend a Catholic Mass or observe other Catholic rituals or ceremonies. As my family of origin were still practicing Catholics, all family weddings and funerals were held in Catholic churches. Each of those events became times of much internal struggle for me. At times I was able to hold my anger in check, while at other times I was not able to do this.

It eventually became clear to me that I needed to make peace with the Catholic Church if I were to grow in faith and truly walk the walk. With God's help I was able to accomplish this by learning to see the cup as half full rather than half empty. I began to look with appreciation at what the church did do, rather than look with anger at what it didn't do. What the Catholic Church did do is this: teach me that God exists, that he made me, and that spiritual matters are important. The church also instilled in me a belief that church is where one develops good morals. If it were not for this last lesson, I would never have brought my children to church and would never have been led into a relationship with the real God.

I am now at a place in my faith journey where I am grateful to the Catholic Church for what it did teach me. Though anger at the church still rears its ugly head from time to time, it is quickly replaced by a deep sadness for the multitude of faithful Catholics who do not know the joy and peace of resting in the certainty of their salvation and the unconditional love of their heavenly Father. At the same time, I am extremely grateful to God for leading me away from the Catholic Church and teaching me that it is not about religion; it's about relationship.

I am ending this book with a link to another of my favorite songs. I encourage you to listen to Fernando Ortega's "Give Me Jesus" at https://www.youtube.com/watch?v=l1O_Jf_fdkI

THE TEN COMMANDMENTS

Exodus 20:2–17

"I am the LORD your God, who rescued you from the land of Egypt, the place of your slavery.

"You must not have any other god but me.

"You must not make for yourself an idol of any kind or an image of anything in the heavens or on the earth or in the sea. You must not bow down to them or worship them, for I, the LORD your God, am a jealous God who will not tolerate your affection for any other gods. I lay the sins of the parents upon their children; the entire family is affected— even children in the third and fourth generations of those who reject me. But I lavish unfailing love for a thousand generations on those who love me and obey my commands.

"You must not misuse the name of the LORD your God. The LORD will not let you go unpunished if you misuse his name.

"Remember to observe the Sabbath day by keeping it holy. You have six days each week for your ordinary work, but the seventh day is a Sabbath day of rest dedicated to the LORD your God. On that day no one in your household may do any work. This includes you, your sons and daughters, your male and female servants, your livestock, and any foreigners living among you. For in six days the LORD made the heavens, the earth, the sea, and everything in them; but on the seventh day he rested. That is why the LORD blessed the Sabbath day and set it apart as holy.

"Honor your father and mother. Then you will live a long, full life in the land the LORD your God is giving you.

"You must not murder.

"You must not commit adultery.

"You must not steal.

"You must not testify falsely against your neighbor.

"You must not covet your neighbor's house. You must not covet your neighbor's wife, male or female servant, ox or donkey, or anything else that belongs to your neighbor."

THE SERMON ON THE MOUNT

Matthew 5:1—7:29

One day as he saw the crowds gathering, Jesus went up on the mountainside and sat down. His disciples gathered around him, and he began to teach them.

The Beatitudes

"God blesses those who are poor and realize their need for him,
for the Kingdom of Heaven is theirs.
God blesses those who mourn,
for they will be comforted.
God blesses those who are humble,
for they will inherit the whole earth.
God blesses those who hunger and thirst for justice,
for they will be satisfied.
God blesses those who are merciful,
for they will be shown mercy.
God blesses those whose hearts are pure,
for they will see God.

God blesses those who work for peace,
for they will be called the children of God.
God blesses those who are persecuted for doing right,
for the Kingdom of Heaven is theirs.

"God blesses you when people mock you and persecute you and lie about you and say all sorts of evil things against you because you are my followers. Be happy about it! Be very glad! For a great reward awaits you in heaven. And remember, the ancient prophets were persecuted in the same way.

Teaching about Salt and Light

"You are the salt of the earth. But what good is salt if it has lost its flavor? Can you make it salty again? It will be thrown out and trampled underfoot as worthless.

"You are the light of the world—like a city on a hilltop that cannot be hidden. No one lights a lamp and then puts it under a basket. Instead, a lamp is placed on a stand, where it gives light to everyone in the house. In the same way, let your good deeds shine out for all to see, so that everyone will praise your heavenly Father.

Teaching about the Law

"Don't misunderstand why I have come. I did not come to abolish the law of Moses or the writings of the prophets. No, I came to accomplish their purpose. I tell you the truth, until heaven and earth disappear, not even the smallest detail of God's law will disappear until its purpose is achieved. So if you ignore the least commandment and teach others to do the same, you will be called the least in the Kingdom of Heaven. But anyone who obeys God's laws and teaches them will be called great in the Kingdom of Heaven.

"But I warn you—unless your righteousness is better than the righteousness of the teachers of religious law and the Pharisees, you will never enter the Kingdom of Heaven!

Teaching about Anger

"You have heard that our ancestors were told, 'You must not murder. If you commit murder, you are subject to judgment.' But I say, if you are even angry with someone, you are subject to judgment! If you call someone an idiot, you are in danger of being brought before the court. And if you curse someone, you are in danger of the fires of hell.

"So if you are presenting a sacrifice at the altar in the Temple and you suddenly remember that someone has something against you, leave your sacrifice there at the altar. Go and be reconciled to that person. Then come and offer your sacrifice to God.

"When you are on the way to court with your adversary, settle your differences quickly. Otherwise, your accuser may hand you over to the judge, who will hand you over to an officer, and you will be thrown into prison. And if that happens, you surely won't be free again until you have paid the last penny.

Teaching about Adultery

"You have heard the commandment that says, 'You must not commit adultery.' But I say, anyone who even looks at a woman with lust has already committed adultery with her in his heart. So if your eye—even your good eye—causes you to lust, gouge it out and throw it away. It is better for you to lose one part of your body than for your whole body to be thrown into hell. And if your hand—even your stronger hand—causes you to sin, cut it off and throw it away. It is better for you to lose one part of your body than for your whole body to be thrown into hell.

Teaching about Divorce

"You have heard the law that says, 'A man can divorce his wife by merely giving her a written notice of divorce.' But I say that a man who divorces his wife, unless she has been unfaithful, causes her to commit adultery. And anyone who marries a divorced woman also commits adultery.

Teaching about Vows

"You have also heard that our ancestors were told, 'You must not break your vows; you must carry out the vows you make to the Lord.' But I say, do not make any vows! Do not say, 'By heaven!' because heaven is God's throne. And do not say, 'By the earth!' because the earth is his footstool. And do not say, 'By Jerusalem!' for Jerusalem is the city of the great King. Do not even say, 'By my head!' for you can't turn one hair white or black. Just say a simple, 'Yes, I will,' or 'No, I won't.' Anything beyond this is from the evil one.

Teaching about Revenge

"You have heard the law that says the punishment must match the injury: 'An eye for an eye, and a tooth for a tooth.' But I say, do not resist an evil person! If someone slaps you on the right cheek, offer the other cheek also. If you are sued in court and your shirt is taken from you, give your coat, too. If a soldier demands that you carry his gear for a mile, carry it two miles. Give to those who ask, and don't turn away from those who want to borrow.

Teaching about Love for Enemies

"You have heard the law that says, 'Love your neighbor' and hate your enemy. But I say, love your enemies! Pray for those who persecute you! In that way, you will be acting as true children of your Father in heaven. For he gives his sunlight to both the evil and the good, and he sends rain on the just and the unjust alike. If you love only those who love you, what reward is there for that? Even corrupt tax collectors do that much. If you are kind only to your friends, how are you different than anyone else? Even pagans do that. But you are to be perfect, even as your Father in heaven is perfect.

Teaching about Giving to the Needy

"Watch out! Don't do your good deeds publicly, to be admired by others, for you will lose the reward from your Father in heaven. When you give to someone in need, don't do as the hypocrites do—blowing trumpets in the synagogues and streets to call attention to their acts of charity! I tell you the truth, they have received all the reward they will ever get. But when you give to someone in need, don't let your left hand know what your right hand is doing. Give your gifts in private, and your Father, who sees everything, will reward you.

Teaching about Prayer and Fasting

"When you pray, don't be like the hypocrites who love to pray publicly on street corners and in the synagogues where everyone can see them. I tell you the truth, that is all the reward they will ever get. But when you pray, go away by yourself, shut the door behind you, and pray to your Father in private. Then your Father, who sees everything, will reward you.

"When you pray, don't babble on and on as people of other religions do. They think their prayers are answered merely by repeating their words again and again. Don't be like them, for your Father knows exactly what you need even before you ask him! Pray like this:

Our Father in heaven,
    may your name be kept holy.
May your kingdom come soon.
May your will be done on earth,
    as it is in heaven.
Give us today the food we need,
and forgive us our sins,
    as we have forgiven those who sin against us.
And don't let us yield to temptation,
    but rescue us from the evil one.

"If you forgive those who sin against you, your heavenly Father will forgive you. But if you refuse to forgive others, your Father will not forgive your sins.

"And when you fast, don't make it obvious, as the hypocrites do, for they try to look miserable and disheveled so people will admire them for their fasting. I tell you the truth, that is the only reward they will ever get. But when you fast, comb your hair and wash your face. Then no one will notice that you are fasting, except your Father, who knows what you do in private. And your Father, who sees everything, will reward you.

Teaching about Money and Possessions

"Don't store up treasures here on earth, where moths eat them and rust destroys them, and where thieves break in and steal. Store your treasures in heaven, where moths and rust cannot destroy, and thieves do not break in and steal. Wherever your treasure is, there the desires of your heart will also be.

"Your eye is a lamp that provides light for your body. When your eye is good, your whole body is filled with light. But when your eye is bad, your whole body is filled with darkness. And if the light you think you have is actually darkness, how deep that darkness is!

"No one can serve two masters. For you will hate one and love the other; you will be devoted to one and despise the other. You cannot serve God and be enslaved to money.

"That is why I tell you not to worry about everyday life—whether you have enough food and drink, or enough clothes to wear. Isn't life more than food, and your body more than clothing? Look at the birds. They don't plant or harvest or store food in barns, for your heavenly Father feeds them. And aren't you far more valuable to him than they are? Can all your worries add a single moment to your life?

"And why worry about your clothing? Look at the lilies of the field and how they grow. They don't work or make their clothing, yet Solomon in all his glory was not dressed as beautifully as they are. And if God cares so wonderfully for wildflowers that are here today and thrown into the fire tomorrow, he will certainly care for you. Why do you have so little faith?

"So don't worry about these things, saying, 'What will we eat? What will we drink? What will we wear?' These things dominate the thoughts of unbelievers, but your heavenly Father already knows all your needs. Seek the Kingdom of God above all else, and live righteously, and he will give you everything you need.

"So don't worry about tomorrow, for tomorrow will bring its own worries. Today's trouble is enough for today.

Do Not Judge Others

"Do not judge others, and you will not be judged. For you will be treated as you treat others. The standard you use in judging is the standard by which you will be judged.

"And why worry about a speck in your friend's eye when you have a log in your own? How can you think of saying to your friend, 'Let me help you get rid of that speck in your eye,' when you can't see past the log in your own eye? Hypocrite! First get rid of the log in your own eye; then you will see well enough to deal with the speck in your friend's eye.

"Don't waste what is holy on people who are unholy. Don't throw your pearls to pigs! They will trample the pearls, then turn and attack you.

Effective Prayer

"Keep on asking, and you will receive what you ask for. Keep on seeking, and you will find. Keep on knocking, and the door will be opened to you. For everyone who asks, receives. Everyone who seeks, finds. And to everyone who knocks, the door will be opened.

"You parents—if your children ask for a loaf of bread, do you give them a stone instead? Or if they ask for a fish, do you give them a snake? Of course not! So if you sinful people know how to give good gifts to your children, how much more will your heavenly Father give good gifts to those who ask him.

The Golden Rule

"Do to others whatever you would like them to do to you. This is the essence of all that is taught in the law and the prophets.

The Narrow Gate

"You can enter God's Kingdom only through the narrow gate. The highway to hell is broad, and its gate is wide for the many who choose that way. But the gateway to life is very narrow and the road is difficult, and only a few ever find it.

The Tree and Its Fruit

"Beware of false prophets who come disguised as harmless sheep but are really vicious wolves. You can identify them by their fruit, that is, by the way they act. Can you pick grapes from thornbushes, or figs from thistles? A good tree produces good fruit, and a bad tree produces bad fruit. A good tree can't produce bad fruit, and a bad tree can't produce good fruit. So every tree that does not produce good fruit is chopped down and thrown into the fire. Yes, just as you can identify a tree by its fruit, so you can identify people by their actions.

True Disciples

"Not everyone who calls out to me, 'Lord! Lord!' will enter the Kingdom of Heaven. Only those who actually do the will of my Father in heaven will enter. On judgment day many will say to me, 'Lord! Lord! We prophesied in your name and cast out demons in your name and performed many miracles in your name.' But I will reply, 'I never knew you. Get away from me, you who break God's laws.'

Building on a Solid Foundation

"Anyone who listens to my teaching and follows it is wise, like a person who builds a house on solid rock. Though the rain comes in torrents and the floodwaters rise and the winds beat against that house, it won't collapse because it is built on bedrock. But anyone who hears my teaching and doesn't obey it is foolish, like a person who builds a house on sand. When the rains and floods come and the winds beat against that house, it will collapse with a mighty crash."

When Jesus had finished saying these things the crowds were amazed at his teaching, for he taught with real authority—quite unlike their teachers of religious law.

NOTES

1. Bruxy Cavey, *The End of Religion* (Colorado Springs, Colorado: NavPress, 2007), 37.
2. Ibid., 41.
3. Scot McKnight, *The Blue Parakeet* (Grand Rapids, Michigan: Zondervan, 2008), 169.
4. Richard Byrd Wilke and Julia Kitchens Wilke, *Disciple: Becoming Disciples Through Bible Study, Study Manual* (Abingdon Press, 1993), 103–104.
5. John Fischer, *12 Steps for the Recovering Pharisee (Like Me)* (Minneapolis, Minnesota: Bethany House Publishers, 2000), 10.
6. Bill Hybels, *Too Busy Not to Pray* (Downers Grove, Illinois: InterVarsity Press, 1998), 148.
7. Ibid., 179.
8. Rick Warren, *The Purpose Driven Life* (Grand Rapids, Michigan: Zondervan, 2002), 64.
9. Rick Muchow, *The Worship Answer Book* (Nashville, Tennessee: J. Countryman, a division of Thomas Nelson, Inc., 2006), 7

10. Joyce Meyer, *The Power of Simple Prayer* (New York, New York: FaithWords Hachette Book Group USA, 2007), 92.

11. Ibid., 94.

12. Marcus J. Borg, *Jesus A New Vision* (San Francisco, California: Harper & Row, 1987), 192–193.

13. Gregory A. Boyd, *Repenting of Religion* (Grand Rapids, Michigan: Baker Books, 2004), 54.

14. Bruxy Cavey, *The End of Religion* (Colorado Springs, Colorado: NavPress, 2007), 116–117.

15. Ibid., 82.

16. Rick Warren, *The Purpose Driven Life* (Grand Rapids, Michigan: Zondervan, 2002), 234–235.

17. John C. Maxwell, *Becoming a Person of Influence* (Siloam Springs, Arkansas: Garborgs, a division of DaySpring Cards, Inc., 2003).

18. Bruxy Cavey, *The End of Religion* (Colorado Springs, Colorado: NavPress, 2007), 212–213.

19. Gregory A. Boyd, *Repenting of Religion* (Grand Rapids, Michigan: Baker Books, 2004), 181.

20. Neil T. Anderson, Rich Miller, and Paul Travis, *Breaking the Bondage of Legalism* (Eugene, Oregon: Harvest House Publishers, 2003), 37.

21. Bruxy Cavey, *The End of Religion* (Colorado Springs, Colorado: NavPress, 2007), 65.

22. Henry and Richard Blackaby, *Spiritual Leadership* (Nashville, Tennessee: Broadman & Holman Publishers, 2001), 62.

23. Bruxy Cavey, *The End of Religion* (Colorado Springs, Colorado: NavPress, 2007), 213.

24. Gregory A. Boyd, *Repenting of Religion* (Grand Rapids, Michigan: Baker Books, 2004), 45.
25. Ibid., 181.
26. Bill Hybels, *Courageous Leadership* (Grand Rapids, Michigan: Zondervan, 2002), 22.
27. Bruxy Cavey, *The End of Religion* (Colorado Springs, Colorado: NavPress, 2007), 222–223.
28. John Fischer, *12 Steps for the Recovering Pharisee (Like Me)* (Minneapolis, Minnesota: Bethany House Publishers, 2000), 10.
29. Rick Warren, *The Purpose Driven Life* (Grand Rapids, Michigan: Zondervan, 2002), 241.
30. James G. McCarthy, *The Gospel According to Rome* (Eugene, Oregon: Harvest House Publishers, 1995), 84.
31. Ibid., 85–86.
32. Ibid., 63.
33. Ibid., 55–56.
34. Ibid., 57.
35. Ibid., 63–65.
36. Lewis B. Smedes, *The Art of Forgiving; When You Need to Forgive and Don't Know How* (New York, New York: The Random House Publishing Group, 1996), xii-xiii.
37. Lewis B. Smedes, *Forgive & Forget; Healing the Hurts We Don't Deserve* (New York, New York: HarperCollins Publishers, 1984), 94.